CLONING
SCIENCE & SOCIETY

IDEAS in CONFLICT

Gary E. McCuen

GARY McCUEN
publications inc.

411 Mallalieu Drive
Hudson, Wisconsin 54016
Phone (715) 386-7113

Illustration and Photo Credits

Animal Rights Coalition, Inc. 83, 95, 105; General Board of Church and Society of the United Methodist Church 64; Walt Handlesman 45, 51, 69; National Bioethics Advisory Commission 19, 25, 89, 100; Jack Ohman 59, 73; Star Tribune Graphic, Minneapolis 33; Steve Sack 41.

GEM
ARY McCUEN
publications inc.

© 1998 by Gary E. McCuen Publications, Inc.
411 Mallalieu Drive, Hudson, Wisconsin 54016

(715) 386-7113

International Standard Book Number
0-86596-143-3
Printed in the United States of America

CONTENTS

Ideas in Conflict

Chapter 1   HUMAN CLONING: AN OVERVIEW

Chapter 2   CLONING HUMAN BEINGS

Chapter 3   ANIMAL CLONING

Chapter 4   RELIGIOUS TRADITIONS AND CLONING

a. Native American

b. Buddhism

c. Hinduism

d. Islam

e. Judaism

f. Protestant Christianity: Mainline

g. Protestant Christianity: Conservative Evangelical

h. Roman Catholic Christianity

i. Orthodox Christianity

j. African American Churches

REASONING SKILL DEVELOPMENT

These activities may be used as individualized study guides for students in libraries and resource centers or as discussion catalysts in small group and classroom discussions.

IDEAS
in CONFLICT

This series features ideas in conflict on political, social, and moral issues. It presents counterpoints, debates, opinions, commentary, and analysis for use in libraries and classrooms. Each title in the series uses one or more of the following basic elements:

Introductions *that present an issue overview giving historic background and/or a description of the controversy.*

Counterpoints *and debates carefully chosen from publications, books, and position papers on the political right and left to help librarians and teachers respond to requests that treatment of public issues be fair and balanced.*

Symposiums *and forums that go beyond debates that can polarize and oversimplify. These present commentary from across the political spectrum that reflect how complex issues attract many shades of opinion.*

A *global* *emphasis with foreign perspectives and surveys on various moral questions and political issues that will help readers to place subject matter in a less culture-bound and ethnocentric frame of reference. In an ever-shrinking and interdependent world, understanding and cooperation are essential. Many issues are global in nature and can be effectively dealt with only by common efforts and international understanding.*

Reasoning skill *study guides and discussion activities provide ready-made tools for helping with critical reading and evaluation of content. The guides and activities deal with one or more of the following:*

RECOGNIZING AUTHOR'S POINT OF VIEW

INTERPRETING EDITORIAL CARTOONS

VALUES IN CONFLICT

WHAT IS EDITORIAL BIAS?

WHAT IS SEX BIAS?

WHAT IS POLITICAL BIAS?

WHAT IS ETHNOCENTRIC BIAS?

WHAT IS RACE BIAS?

WHAT IS RELIGIOUS BIAS?

*From across **the political spectrum** varied sources are presented for research projects and classroom discussions. Diverse opinions in the series come from magazines, newspapers, syndicated columnists, books, political speeches, foreign nations, and position papers by corporations and nonprofit institutions.*

About the Editor

Gary E. McCuen is an editor and publisher of anthologies for libraries and discussion materials for schools and colleges. His publications have specialized in social, moral and political conflict. They include books, pamphlets, cassettes, tabloids, filmstrips and simulation games, most of them created from his many years of experience in teaching and educational publishing.

CHAPTER 1

HUMAN CLONING: AN OVERVIEW

READING

1

CLONING AND PUBLIC POLICY

Irene Stith-Coleman

Irene Stith-Coleman is a specialist in Life Sciences with the Science Policy Research Division in the Library of Congress.

■ POINTS TO CONSIDER

1. What was unique about the sheep cloned in Scotland?

2. How did President Clinton respond?

3. Discuss the definition of cloning.

4. Describe the three techniques of cloning.

5. Explain the potential uses of cloning.

6. Summarize the ethical and social issues raised by cloning.

Irene Stith-Coleman, "Cloning: Where Do We Go from Here?" **CRS Report for Congress**, July 21, 1997, p. 1-5.

The possibility of cloning human beings raises profound moral and ethical questions.

Recent news that scientists in Scotland had succeeded in cloning an adult sheep ignited a worldwide debate. Of particular concern are the ethical and social implications of the potential application of cloning techniques to produce human beings. The Scottish announcement marked the first time that researchers were able to produce an exact genetic replica of an adult animal. Scientists have identified a number of potential medical and agricultural applications for this technique. Within hours of the newsbreak, President Clinton asked his National Bioethics Advisory Commission (NBAC) to initiate a complete review of the ethical and social issues related to cloning and report back within 90 days.

On March 4, 1997, the President sent a memorandum to the heads of all executive departments and agencies making it "absolutely clear that no federal funds will be used for human cloning." He also urged the private sector to adopt a voluntary ban on the cloning of humans until the NABC completed its evaluation. Legislation has been introduced in the Senate (S. 368) and House (H.R. 922 and H.R. 923) that would prohibit human cloning research. Hearings have been held on cloning in both chambers. The NBAC presented its report, in which it recommended, among other things, that federal legislation be enacted to prohibit anyone from attempting to create a child through cloning. President Clinton has sent up to Congress legislation (the "Cloning and Prohibition Act of 1997"), which reflects the NBAC recommendations. This report provides information on the major policy issues related to this topic.

BACKGROUND

On February 24, 1997, scientists at the Roslin Institute in Edinburgh, Scotland, announced that they had cloned an adult mammal for the first time. The researchers used the nucleus of a mammary gland cell from an adult sheep and a sheep egg, which had its nucleus removed. The two were fused using electrical pulses; the pulses also prompted the egg to start dividing and form an embryo. The embryo was then transferred to the uterus of a surrogate sheep, where it implanted and grew to term resulting in the birth of a live lamb, Dolly. Analyses of the genetic material confirmed that Dolly was derived from the adult sheep's mammary cell. Before cloning the adult sheep, scientists believed that an early embryo was required as the source of the genetic material for cloning, and that a clone could not be derived from a cell of an adult animal.

The cloning method used to produce Dolly, known as *somatic cell nuclear transfer cloning,* could have a number of significant medical and agriculture applications. Examples include the creation of improved breeds of livestock, development of animals that can produce drugs for use by or whose organs can be used in, humans. In the sheep cloning experiment, the number of embryo implants that resulted in live births was very low. A total of 273 fused eggs were implanted, but only one lamb was born. However, researchers believe that further research will improve the efficiency of the technique. It does not yet appear possible to clone humans. Nevertheless, a major concern of many people, including some who support the cloning of animals, is that this technique could in the future be developed to a point that would make it possible to clone humans.

In response to concerns about the potential application of cloning to produce humans, actions have been taken by the Administration and Congress. President Clinton, on February 24, 1997, asked the NBAC to thoroughly review the ethical and legal issues associated with the use of cloning technology. The Commission reported its findings and recommendations to the President on June 9, 1997. It recommended that federal legislation be enacted to prohibit the use of cloning to create a child in both the public and private sector. The NBAC found it morally unacceptable at this time to attempt to clone humans because current scientific data indicate that the method is not safe.

What is *cloning?* Cloning is defined as making genetically identical copies of a single cell or organism. Before cloning the adult sheep, researchers had created mammalian clones only from embryo cells using one of three techniques: *blastomere separation, blastocyst division and twinning,* or *nuclear transplantation.* For each technique, an embryo is produced by *in vitro fertilization* (IVF), where an egg is fertilized with sperm in a laboratory dish. Once fertilized, the embryo is allowed to divide into a two- to eight-cell stage and then is cloned by one of the three techniques.

In *Blastomere Separation,* the outer coating, or *zone pellucida,* is removed from around a two- to eight-cell embryo, then placed in a special solution that causes the cells, called *blastomeres,* to separate. Each cell can then be cultured individually, because at

11

this stage of embryo development, each cell is "totipotent," that is, it is undifferentiated and can develop into an organism. After dividing a few times, the blastomere develops into a smaller-than-normal embryo that can be transferred to the uterus.

In *Blastocyst Division,* also called induced twinning, an embryo, at the *blastocyst* stage, a more advanced stage of development than the blastomere, is mechanically split into two. The two parts can be transferred to the uterus. If both halves develop, then, at most, one blastocyst gives rise to identical twins.

In *Nuclear Transplantation,* a nucleus is transferred from each blastomere of a four- to eight-cell or later-stage embryo into the cytoplasm (cell contents other than nucleus) of an egg from which the genetic material has been removed (enucleated egg). To do this, the blastomere is placed beside an enucleated egg and their membranes are fused together artificially, for example, with electrical pulses. The nucleus from the blastomere enters the egg cytoplasm and directs development of the embryo.

The Scottish scientists used a variant of the nuclear transplantation technique, where the nucleus that programmed the creation of Dolly was transferred from the adult sheep mammary cell, not from an embryo. Researchers had thought that when cells became differentiated to do certain jobs in the body, they could not revert to the embryo stage. For example, they thought that a cell that became a liver cell remained a liver cell, but that belief was disproven by the Scottish scientists. They were able to reprogram the genes in a mammary gland cell to make it act like an undifferentiated embryo, which then developed into a sheep.

POTENTIAL USES OF CLONING

Cloning conceivably could be used to produce large numbers of genetically identical organisms. However, scientists wish to use it as a research tool to understand how genes in cells can be switched off and on. Each cell in the body (with a few exceptions) has the same genes. One embryo cell becomes mammary tissue and another liver when certain genes are switched on and others switched off. The technique used by the Scottish scientists turned off the genes for mammary function and turned on those that function at the embryo stage. But scientists do not know how the technique worked. When more is known, the hope is that this knowledge can be used for other research, such as growing new skin for burn victims, culturing bone marrow that could be used to treat cancer patients, and manipulating genes to cure sickle cell anemia.

One potential application of cloning human embryos would be in treating infertility. Infertility affects more than 2.8 million U.S. couples. About one-half of those couples eventually conceive with some form of treatment, such as in vitro fertilization (IVF). There have been more than 16,000 IVF births worldwide since 1978, when the first IVF birth, of Louise Brown, occurred in England. However, the overall live-birth rate for IVF is low. Research indicates that if more than one embryo is transferred to the uterus per treatment cycle, the chance that at least one will implant and lead to a live birth increases. However, some patients (for example, older reproductive-age and so-called "poor responder" patients) undergoing IVF, have a limited number of embryos for transfer and implantation. Researchers have suggested that those patients could benefit from having their embryos cloned. However, it is unclear that embryo cloning would help in these cases, because the quality of the embryos from such patients also tends to be diminished.

ETHICAL AND SOCIAL ISSUES

The possibility of cloning human beings raises profound moral and ethical questions. No scientific rationale has yet been identified for cloning an existing human. A major concern is that cloning would seriously affect society's perception of what it means to be a human being. There are also unanswered questions about a cloned individual's personal identity, uniqueness, and individuality. Many worry that cloning would lead to diminished respect for humans in general, and for cloned individuals, in particular, since the cloned person could simply be replaced with another clone. Others point out that does not occur today with twins.

In addition to possible problems related to individuality, identity, and human values, cloning human embryos raises difficult questions about the rights of parents to control their own embryos, other issues in reproductive rights, and privacy. Some observers believe that it would be ethical to clone human embryos to help infertile couples conceive in an IVF setting. For example, some believe that the technique, if perfected, could be used by parents to grow one embryo to term and store (by freezing) the others indefinitely. Later, one of these spare embryos could be thawed, transferred, implanted, and grown to term, where it would become an identical, but younger, twin of the first sibling. Many are concerned, however, that the production of a human clone of an existing embryo would be counter to human values as civilization has defined them.

Some parents might want to store embryo clones as a backup in case their child died, or so that if their child needed an organ or tissue transplant, such as bone marrow, the mother could give birth to the child's identical twin. Others argue that the use of clones as potential sources of tissue or organs would be unethical. The National Advisory Board on Ethics in Reproduction (NABER) has recommended that legislation be enacted to ban the commercial use of human embryos.

THE LEGAL STATUS OF CLONING

National Bioethics Advisory Commission

The National Bioethics Advisory Commission is a Presidential advisory group that makes national policy recommendations on difficult bioethical issues like cloning. After meeting and consulting with ethicists, theologians, scientists, physicians, politicians and other citizens, the advisory commission published a report to the Nation titled Cloning Human Beings. *The following article is taken from this report.*

■ POINTS TO CONSIDER

1. Describe the federal law that would affect efforts to clone human beings.

2. How do state laws relate to cloning?

3. How are liberty and freedom limited in American tradition?

4. Explain the difference between an ordinary individual liberty and a more important fundamental kind of right.

5. Do you think cloning a human being should be viewed as procreation or replication?

Excerpted from "Cloning Human Beings," **Report and Recommendations of the National Bioethics Advisory Commission**, June 1997.

Some argue that if the method can be used as a means to serve reproductive ends, it should be classified as procreation. Others disagree, deeming cloning with somatic cell nuclear transfer to represent a radical new step that should be classified as "replication," rather than "reproduction."

Almost immediately after the announcement of Dolly's birth, legislation was introduced in the Congress and in approximately a dozen states, aimed at prohibiting all or some research on human cloning. At present, there is no law in the United States directly addressing attempts to create a child through somatic cell nuclear transfer, although a variety of state and federal laws and policies do have some application.

FEDERAL LAW

Federal law already requires that clinics using assisted reproduction techniques, such as in vitro fertilization, be monitored. The requirement would appear to apply, as well, to efforts to use somatic cell nuclear transfer cloning to create a child. This statute, the Fertility Clinic Success Rate and Certification Act of 1992, covers all laboratories and treatments that involve manipulation of human eggs and embryos, and requires that rates of success at achieving pregnancies be reported to the Department of Health and Human Services (DHHS) for publication in a consumer guide. It also directs DHHS to develop a model program for inspection and certification of laboratories that use human embryos, to be implemented by the states.

As this statute is implemented, any clinic or laboratory involved in attempts to initiate pregnancies by somatic cell nuclear transfer cloning, should be identifiable to the federal government, and the outcomes of its efforts known to the public. As states move to implement the inspection and certification aspects of the law, a mechanism would exist to prevent attempts to use cloning, if it is shown to be ineffective or dangerous for the tissue donor or resulting child.

Federal regulations governing the use of human beings in research also restrict the conduct or funding of any research aimed at cloning human beings. Enforcement lies primarily in the hands of "Institutional Review Boards" (IRBs), committees appointed by institutions (such as universities) where research is conducted. IRBs review experiments before people can be enrolled. To the extent that efforts to clone human beings take place at institutions funded by the federal government, any serious question about the physical harms that might result would make it difficult for such experimentation to be approved.

National Institutes of Health (NIH) should not finance any research that involves creating embryos solely for research that would result in their destruction. Furthermore, Congress has passed prohibitions on the use of FY96 and FY97 funds appropriated to the Departments of Labor, Education, and Health and Human Services for any research that involves exposing embryos to risk of destruction for non-therapeutic research. The net effect of these policies is to eliminate virtually all federal funding for research to perfect methods for cloning human beings.

STATE LAWS

While these restrictions prohibit only federally funded research, a number of state laws regarding the management of embryos arguably could restrict even privately funded research. By and large, however, states do not have legislation directly regulating assisted reproduction techniques, leaving state medical malpractice law as the primary means for regulating clinical application of the technology.

State laws governing family relationships would also be applicable if efforts to clone human beings were successful. But paternity acts, surrogacy statutes, and egg donation statutes are not necessarily broad enough to address the kinship relationships involved in cloning human beings. The use of this technique would result in a child having as many as four individuals with claims to parental status based on some aspect of genetic connection: the person from whom the cell nucleus was derived, that individual's genetic parents, and the woman contributing the enucleated egg cell which contains a small fraction of DNA in the cytoplasmic mitochondria. In addition, if the egg with the transferred nucleic material is implanted in a gestational mother, the child will have two other potential parents: the gestational mother, and if she is married, her husband. Finally, the intended rearing parents could be unrelated to the individuals whose egg or nucleus was used, or to the gestational mother. The contributors to such cloning arrangements will have various, as yet ill-defined, legal rights and responsibilities with respect to the resulting child.

Overall, existing law would severely restrict public funding for efforts to clone human beings; would monitor most efforts to clone human beings for safety and efficacy; and would discourage premature experimentation. It would not, however, prohibit all such efforts. Further, if an attempt to clone a human being were successful, then existing law would struggle to characterize the family relationships that ensue.

LIBERTY AND LIMITED FEDERAL POWERS

The presumption in favor of individual freedom of action cannot be interpreted simplistically. From the writings of Locke to the writings of the United States Supreme Court, the American tradition has been to assume a freedom to act, absent a specific, justifiable prohibition. This tradition is enshrined in the Constitutional language of liberty used in case law, ranging from freedom from unreasonable searches and seizures to freedom to refuse medical treatment. But the liberty enshrined in American tradition and Constitutional law is not unfettered; rather, it is the ordered liberty of a social compact. To ensure the good order of society, one person's liberty may be limited when its exercise would limit the liberty of another, or would otherwise undermine important social values.

It is for this reason that an individual's actions may be limited when they would directly harm another. This principle can be applied even when the harm will not be experienced by a currently living person. Thus, on occasion, American courts have recognized that even actions taken prior to the conception of a child might lead to legal responsibility for that child's health costs, if the actions were unreasonable and avoidable.

On this basis alone, efforts at this time to create a child via somatic cell nuclear transfer may well be inappropriate, since there is widespread consensus that such a step would be dangerous and premature before a great deal of further animal research is conducted.

MORALITY AND PUBLIC POLICY FORMATION

Concerns about the potential impact of cloning human beings through somatic cell nuclear transfer on public and private values and morale are quite real, but nonetheless difficult to articulate with precision. These ethical and theological concerns focus on

18

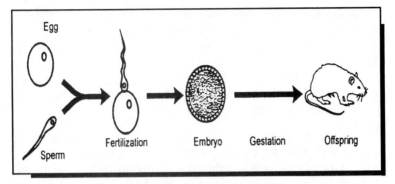

Sexual reproduction. Source: National Bioethics Advisory Commission.

effects on self-identity, human dignity, privacy, autonomy, and kinship relations.

Americans share some but not all of their ethical and cultural traditions, and no single set of approaches that balances conflicting values in particular ways enjoys universal acceptance. Some theological analyses provide answers to their adherents, but these are incapable of serving as the sole basis for policy making in a religiously diverse nation committed to separation of church and state. Further, the absence of an agreed upon methodology in moral philosophy or bioethics for resolving disputes among competing ethical theories and conflicting values means that no analytical argument can be persuasive to every person. Nonetheless, the instinctive distrust with which much of the American public greeted the prospect of cloning is necessarily a significant factor. No suggested public policy can hope to gather support and compliance in the absence of either consensus or persuasive argumentation.

FUNDAMENTAL LIBERTIES, PROCREATION AND CLONING

While arguments may make a strong political case for prohibiting cloning, American law occasionally demands more. Specifically, while any rational reason will suffice for government limitation of ordinary individual liberties, such as the right to drive or to operate a business, the Constitution demands a more compelling reason when a more important kind of right is infringed upon. Then, any limitation must serve a compelling purpose and must be drawn as narrowly as possible, so as to infringe upon individuals only as needed.

This is the case when fundamental liberties are at stake. Fundamental liberties have been defined by the Supreme Court as those that are specifically mentioned in the Constitution, for example, the right to free speech; those so deeply rooted in our culture and history as to be assumed by the public as beyond casual governmental interference; and those that are so basic they are necessary to a system of ordered liberty.

Thus, to determine if the arguments put forth are sufficient to justify a prohibition constitutionally, as well as politically, it is necessary to examine whether the choice to create a child via somatic cell nuclear transfer cloning would be viewed as a fundamental liberty. Since such cloning, if successful, would involve bringing children into the world, it is quite possible that one could characterize it as a form of procreation, for which the courts have carved out large areas of special protection, since the "bearing and begetting" of children has been characterized as a fundamental right.

The right to make decisions about whether or not to bear children was first constitutionally protected under the constitutional right to privacy. More recently, the Court has reaffirmed the "recognized protection accorded to liberty relating to intimate relationships, the family, and decisions about whether to bear and beget a child." A federal district court has interpreted this right to make procreative decisions to include the right of an infertile couple to undergo medically assisted reproduction, including in vitro fertilization and the use of a donated embryo, stating:

"It takes no great leap of logic to see that within the cluster of constitutionally protected choices that includes the right to have access to contraceptives, there must be included within that cluster, the right to submit to a medical procedure that may bring about, rather than prevent, pregnancy."

Others take a narrower view of the Supreme Court's decisions about reproductive liberty. In this view, the Court merely aimed to protect bodily integrity from direct interference by the state (which would occur if the state compelled or prohibited abortions or contraceptive use) and particularly to ensure that the law not unduly burden women's choices. Thus interpreted, the Constitution would not guarantee individuals unfettered access to assisted reproductive technologies.

Commentators arguing over whether the Constitution should be interpreted to protect the right to create a child through somatic cell nuclear transfer thus begin by debating the present scope of procreative liberty, and then addressing whether or not this method is qualitatively different from existing forms of medically assisted reproduction. Some argue that if the method can be used as a means to serve reproductive ends, it should be classified as procreation. Others disagree, deeming cloning with somatic cell nuclear transfer to represent a radical new step that should be classified as "replication," rather than "reproduction."

To the extent that cloning invokes the choice to generate a child, it is indeed procreative. On the other hand, cases discussing procreative rights have always been premised on underlying assumptions about the meaning of procreation, for example, that it is interdependent, involving the reproductive cooperation of a male and a female, at least on the biological level. Another assumption has been that it involves the transmission of genes vertically across a generation, that is, between a parent and child. Cloning via somatic cell nuclear transfer represents a form of genetic duplication within an existing generation.

Whether cloning is best characterized as procreation or as something entirely new and different, is a matter of debate, for which existing decisions by the U.S. Supreme Court offer only partial guidance. Thus, it is impossible to say with certainty whether somatic cell nuclear transfer cloning would be treated in law as a fundamental right. But if it were to be treated as a fundamental right, then arguments against the practice based on speculative psychological and social harms would be tested against the strictest scrutiny of the judicial system.

READING

3

AN INTERNATIONAL PERSPECTIVE

Bartha Maria Knoppers

Bartha Maria Knoppers is a professor of law and a senior researcher on the faculty of law at the University of Montreal, Canada.

■ POINTS TO CONSIDER

1. Identify the international ethics committees described by the author.

2. What positions do they take on cloning?

3. Summarize the attitude toward cloning by the European Parliament of the European Union.

4. Compare the position toward cloning of the European Parliament with the position of the international non-governmental organizations (NGOs).

Excerpted from Bartha Maria Knoppers, "Cloning: An International Comparative Overview," 1997. This paper was commissioned by the U.S. National Bioethics Advisory Commission.

The stated object of the majority is to protect the dignity of all persons in relation to uses of human genetic materials.

Recently, two international ethics committees, one governmental (UNESCO) and the other non-governmental (HUGO) were deliberately created for the study of the ethical, legal and social issues surrounding human genetics. Neither has an explicit statement on cloning. The UNESCO International Bioethics Committee has as its mandate: "the preparation of an international instrument on the protection of the human genome" (1993).

The preamble of UNESCO's proposed Universal Declaration on the Human Genome and the Protection of Human Rights recalls the universal principles of human rights as found in the international instruments and recognizes that: "research on the human genome and the resulting applications open up vast prospects for progress in improving the health of individuals and of humankind as a whole, but emphasizes that such research should fully respect human dignity and individual rights, as well as the prohibition of all forms of discrimination based on genetic characteristics." In particular, Article 4 foresees the need for scientific research but such research should have therapeutic aims. It provides that: "research, which is necessary to the progress of knowledge, is part of the freedom of thought. Its applications, especially in biology and genetics, should relieve suffering and improve the health of individuals and the well-being of humankind as a whole" and that "benefits from advances in biology and genetics should be made available to all, with due regard to the dignity and rights of each individual." Moreover, Article 5 maintains that: "no research applications should be allowed to prevail over the respect for human dignity and human rights, in particular in the fields of biology and genetics." These provisions taken together would disallow any form of genetic research such as cloning, when interpreted by a signatory country to run afoul of their purpose and scope...

INTERNATIONAL APPROACHES

The International Ethics Committee of HUGO in its Statement on the Principled Conduct of Genetic Research was also concerned with research under the Human Genome Project and Human Genome Diversity Project generally, and not with any particular form of research. However, the Statement in its background principles refers to the "acceptance and upholding of human dignity and freedom." The deliberate creation of a clone could well fall within the purview of concerns...

While easily dismissed as too broad and vague, these international approaches which are necessarily the result of compromise may prove to be more inclusive than the narrow, scientific definitions often found under national legislation.

Turning to the Council of Europe and then to the European Union, November 26, 1996 saw the adoption by the Council of Europe (40 countries) of the Convention for the Protection of Human Rights and Dignity of the Human Being with Regard to the Application of Biology and Medicine: Convention on Human Rights and Biomedicine. Upon signature, this Convention is binding upon member states. Again, even though there is a chapter on the "Human Genome" (Chapter 4), no mention is made of cloning. Article 2 of the Convention however states:

"Parties to this Convention shall protect the dignity and identity of all human beings and guarantee everyone, without discrimination, respect for their integrity and other rights and fundamental freedoms with regard to the application of biology and medicine." Moreover, like the proposed UNESCO Declaration, "scientific research in the field of biology and medicine shall be carried out freely, subject to the provisions of this Convention and the other legal provisions ensuring the protection of the human being" (Article 15).

It is also important to note that earlier recommendations of the Council of Europe either covered medical research and reproductive technologies in general or were "subject specific," that is covered cloning. Beginning with the latter, that is medical research with human beings, in 1990, the Council stated in its preamble to Medical Research on Human Beings, that "...medical research should never be carried out contrary to human dignity"...

Turning now to the resolutions of the European Parliament of the European Union, the first "Resolution on the ethical and legal problems of genetic engineering" was adopted in 1989. It maintained that "the European Parliament as regards clones, considers that the only possible response to the possibility of producing humans by cloning and to experiments with a view to the cloning of humans must be to make them a criminal offense" (Article 41). Then again, in 1994, in Resolution 1235 on Psychiatry and Human Rights, the Parliament asked that "techniques for cloning" be prohibited (Article 13 III[b]).

24

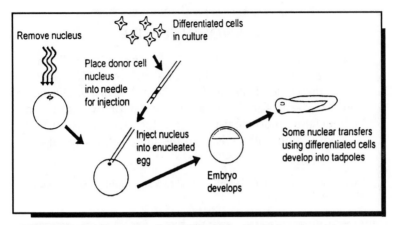

Nuclear transfer carried out in frogs. Source: National Bioethics Advisory Commission.

NGOs

Finally, three statements of international non-governmental organizations (NGOs) bear mention here. The first is that of the International Law Association in its 1988 "Resolution on Reproductive Technologies and the Protection of the Human Person." The position of the Association was that "considering the dignity inherent in all human beings," "any research or manipulation of human genetic material shall be for therapeutic purposes and shall be subject to the approval and control of an ethics committee" (Article 1). Penal sanctions were asked for. Similarly, the 93rd Inter-Parliamentary Conference of 1995, in its wish to promote "universal principles and rights" mentioned "the inviolability of the human body and the intangibility of the genetic heritage of the human species." Finally, the 1996 Charter on Sexual and Reproductive Rights of the International Planned Parenthood Federation (IPPF) also mentions the right to human dignity and access to "safe" and "acceptable" reproduction technologies (Article 103) without further definition.

At the international level then, there is no doubt that respect for human dignity and respect for the intangibility of the human body, its constituent parts and for reproductive tissues and even down to the cells are irreparably linked. While the need for, and value of, research involving humans are reaffirmed, both the proposed UNESCO Declaration and the European Convention would limit such research in the "genetic arena" to therapeutic interventions. These two overarching instruments implicitly refute human

25

UNKNOWN FUTURE

No one knows where the science of cloning will lead. Efforts to replicate the cloning done in Scotland are underway in the United States and elsewhere. The first application could come in farm animals in a year or two, said Ian Wilmut, the embryologist who led the research team that created a lamb with cells from the udder of a six-year-old ewe.

Sharon Schmickle, "Of Cloning, Mortality and Morality," **Star Tribune**, March 16, 1997, p. 1.

cloning. This is not only underscored by the more specific prohibitions on cloning as found in the Recommendations and Resolutions just examined but by national positions.

NATIONAL POSITIONS

It is important to emphasize that like the international instruments just examined, the objectives of national positions are largely similar. Indeed, the stated object of the majority is to protect the dignity of all persons in relation to uses of human genetic materials. Cloning is seen as "diminishing the value of human individuality" and as "violating basic norms of respect for human life" and the "integrity of the human species".

WHAT IS EDITORIAL BIAS?

This activity may be used as an individualized study guide for students in libraries and resource centers or as a discussion catalyst in small group and classroom discussions.

The capacity to recognize an author's point of view is an essential reading skill. The skill to read with insight and understanding involves the ability to detect different kinds of opinions or bias. **Sex bias, race bias, ethnocentric bias, political bias,** and **religious bias** are five basic kinds of opinions expressed in editorials and all literature that attempts to persuade. They are briefly defined below.

Five Kinds of Editorial Opinion or Bias

Sex Bias — The expression of dislike for and/or feeling of superiority over the opposite sex or a particular sexual minority.

Race Bias — The expression of dislike for and/or feeling of superiority over a racial group.

Ethnocentric Bias — The expression of a belief that one's own group, race, religion, culture, or nation is superior. Ethnocentric persons judge others by their own standards and values.

Political Bias — The expression of political opinions and attitudes about domestic or foreign affairs.

Religious Bias — The expression of a religious belief or attitude.

Guidelines

1. From the readings in Chapter One, locate five sentences that provide examples of *editorial opinion* or *bias.*

2. Write down each of the above sentences and determine what kind of bias each sentence represents. Is it *sex bias, race bias, ethnocentric bias, political bias,* or *religious bias?*

3. Make up a one-sentence statement that would be an example of each of the following: *sex bias, race bias, ethnocentric bias, political bias,* and *religious bias.*

4. See if you can locate five sentences that are factual statements from the readings in Chapter One.

CHAPTER 2

CLONING HUMAN BEINGS

READING

4

ADULT CELL CLONING AND EMBRYO SPLITTING: AN OVERVIEW

Karen H. Rothenberg

Karen H. Rothenberg is the Marjorie Cook Professor of Law and the Director of the Law and Health Care Program at the University of Maryland School of Law in Baltimore.

■ POINTS TO CONSIDER

1. Describe the distinctive features of adult cell cloning.

2. How is embryo splitting different from adult cell cloning?

3. Identify the clinical applications of embryo splitting that were found to be unethical by the National Advisory Board on Ethics in Reproduction (NABER).

4. Which clinical applications were found to be ethical?

5. What public policy questions are raised by adult cell cloning?

6. Which one do you think is most important?

Excerpted from testimony by Karen H. Rothenberg before the Subcommittee on Public Health and Safety of the Senate Committee on Labor and Human Resources, March 12, 1997.

Embryo splitting is an in vitro replica of the natural process by which identical twins are created.

I will identify three features of adult cell cloning that distinguish it from previous innovations in reproductive technology, and I will examine how these three features specifically challenge concepts that are central to our understanding of ourselves as persons. Second, I will look at the ethical dilemmas presented by adult human cloning in relation to prior ethical reflection on cloning, most specifically that contained in the *National Advisory Board on Ethics in Reproduction* (NABER) 1994 Report on Human Cloning through Embryo Splitting. I will close by describing the public policy questions raised distinctively by human cloning, noting those of special importance to the federal government.

A. DISTINCTIVE FEATURES OF ADULT CELL CLONING

(1) *Interdependence:* Adult cell cloning requires only one progenitor. Theoretically, a child could be conceived and carried by one person. A woman could have one of her adult cells fused with one of her own unfertilized eggs from which the nucleus had been removed. The resulting embryo could be implanted in her womb and carried to term.

This scenario is unique to adult cell cloning. It is disquieting because it undermines our concept of human beings as fundamentally interrelated, our concept of human interdependence. The fact that the propagation of the species takes two – whether in a test tube or a bedroom – humbles us because it means that practically and symbolically human survival is dependent upon human connectedness.

(2) *Indeterminateness:* In adult cell cloning, we may choose which adult cell to clone based on knowledge of the "expression" of that cell's genetic material in a living, breathing person. Unlike reproductive technology involving only embryos, the cloning of adult cells permits us to see a grown manifestation of the genetic material we are cloning. That knowledge makes genetic selection possible. It creates a choice as to whether to clone the genetic material of person A or person B, Mother Teresa or Madonna, Jesse Jackson or Jesse Helms.

Such choices feel impossible to fathom. Even if we know that we are cloning a person's genetic material and not that person *per se,* the knowing choice of A over B removes some measure of the miraculous variability of the procreative process. Adult cell cloning requires complete human control of conception and legitimizes judgments about the value of all genetically determined traits. It undermines our concept of human beings as diverse creatures.

(3) *Individuality:* Adult cell cloning opens the possibility of creating an infinite number of genetically identical persons. Because the nucleus of every cell in a human body contains the same genetic material, this "raw material" is in infinite supply. Theoretically, the genetic material of any one person could be cloned virtually an infinite number of times.

While variations in gestational environment and upbringing ensure that the cloning of identical genetic material does not result in identical persons, the theoretical possibility of creating hundreds of genetically identical humans is disquieting, if not downright creepy. While I still feel unique if I have one twin sister, I do not if I have 50 or 100. I no longer understand myself as a creation, but as a copy. Adult cell cloning undermines our conception of a human being's individuality.

Given these distinctive features of adult cell cloning, a discussion of the ethical implications must make sense of the challenges these features make to our humanity, that is, to our sense of interdependence, indeterminateness, and individuality.

B. ADULT CELL CLONING IN THE CONTEXT OF PRIOR ETHICAL ANALYSIS

Three years ago, the *National Advisory Board on Ethics in Reproduction* (NABER), a non-governmental, non-profit organization of scientists, ethicists, theologians, and lawyers, investigated the ethical and public policy issues surrounding human cloning through embryo splitting. This investigation was spurred, in large measure, by the announcement that researchers at George Washington University had successfully formed multiple copies of human embryos from a single embryo, using the technique of embryo splitting. Unlike the adult cell cloning technique used by Dr. Wilmut and his colleagues, embryo splitting uses as its "raw material" an embryo, rather than an adult cell. In embryo splitting, clusters of cells of very early embryos are separated and grown

32

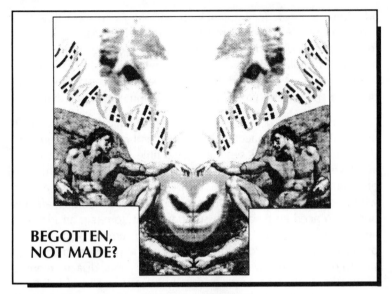

BEGOTTEN, NOT MADE?

into individual embryos. Cells at this state have not yet begun to differentiate into specific tissues, such as bone or muscle, and therefore carry their full genetic complement for development. Each separated embryo may therefore be implanted and carried to term. In effect, embryo splitting is an *in vitro* replica of the natural process by which identical twins are created.

Embryo splitting does not share the three features of adult cell cloning outlined above. First, embryo splitting requires human embryos which must have been created by the fertilization of an egg by a sperm. Second, because only embryos are used, embryo splitting does not provide those involved with the same knowledge of an adult expression of the genetic material. Finally, embryo splitting can produce only a limited number of duplicates of the original. Arguably then, because embryo splitting mimics a natural biological process, it may not present the same challenge to the fundamental human concepts of interdependence, indeterminateness and individuality.

It may not be surprising then that NABER found human embryo splitting ethical in some contexts. NABER's ethical analysis of embryo splitting turned on the question of the specific motivation of a given clinical application. NABER members agreed that human embryo splitting was permissible to improve the chance of initiating pregnancy with in vitro fertilization (IVF) by creating additional embryos for implantation, so long as no more than four identical embryos were produced. Similarly, NABER members found it permissible to use embryo splitting to create embryos to be frozen and implanted at a later date, should the first IVF cycle fail. NABER members disagreed, however, over the acceptability of producing identical embryos for pre-implantation genetic screening.

All other clinical applications were found ethically unacceptable by NABER. It was unacceptable to use embryo splitting solely to produce identical twins separated by a time interval, to provide an adult with an identical twin to raise as his or her own child, to provide an identical embryo as a potential replacement for a child who dies, to create embryos to save for future use should an already born twin need an organ or tissue transplant, to retain an identical embryo as a potential source of fetal tissue, organs or ovaries, to produce embryos for donation to others and to produce embryos for sale to others. There was, however, in many cases, disagreement as to whether embryos that were already created as part of IVF treatment could be used for some of these reasons.

Regardless of whether NABER was correct concerning the morality of embryo splitting for use in fertility treatment, its analysis may not apply with equal force to adult cell cloning. These two cloning techniques, however, do draw into focus the core ethical question: on what grounds is the potential benefit of a scientific innovation outweighed by its potential injury to our concept of what it means to be human? Beyond the hyperbole and fantastic scenarios, that is the ethical dilemma Dolly presents.

C. PUBLIC POLICY QUESTIONS RAISED BY ADULT CELL CLONING

Various public policy questions emerge from the ethical challenge adult cell cloning poses for our society:

1. Fortunately, human cloning will not proceed for some time. The technique would require subjecting unconsenting humans to the unknown effects of "aged" DNA and risk of harm to future children. Nor is there any public support, even from the biotech industry, for moving forward with human cloning at this time. What are the appropriate public policy approaches regarding humans while the technology is just emerging in animals?

2. The federal government has formulated numerous policy responses to emergent reproductive technologies and genetic therapies. For example, the 1994 Report by the National Institutes of Health (NIH) Human Embryo Research Panel articulated ethical considerations to determine what types of research, including cloning, were unacceptable for federal funding. Also, Congress condemned as unethical a market for human organs and fetal tissue. Federal law prohibits their purchase and sale through the National Organ Transplantation Act and the Public Health Service Act. In addition, non-governmental groups, like NABER, have developed perspectives on related issues. What policy guidelines developed in these other contexts are applicable to cloning?

3. Prenatal genetic testing presents couples with difficult questions when serious genetic disorders are discovered *in utero.* Genetic testing may force a kind of "genetic accountability" on women and devalue the lives of people with disabilities. Cloning escalates the genetic screening and genetic selectivity now available. How does cloning fit within the continuum of genetic selectivity already in practice?

4. Cloning presents particular ethical and policy dilemmas when combined with genetic engineering. Because cloning permits us to know a full grown "expression" of the genetic material, when combined with genetic engineering, it allows us to "tinker" with perfecting a person to a degree not previously possible. How should policy decisions regarding adult cloning affect federal policy regarding genetic engineering and enhancement?

5. Adult cloning affects men and women differently. Theoretically, men are not necessary to "conception" by cloning;

35

women are. This fundamental reorientation of sex roles from pro-creation to replication has far reaching consequences for gender roles, and reproductive and parental rights. How should any proposed federal regulation take account of gender differences in how the cloning technique operates?

6. Adult cell cloning upsets our notion of familial relationships. Creation of a child by cloning requires the contribution of DNA material, an unfertilized egg and a ready womb. What language will we use to describe this "family?" By what criteria will we determine the claim of parental status of each of the contributors to the cloning process?

7. Cloning may involve the use of a surrogate. Surrogacy is unregulated on the federal level and remains subject to a confusing patchwork of state statutes and contract principles. Given that the absence of uniform regulation of new reproductive technologies has resulted in such confusion, do the particular features of adult cloning call for federal guidelines?

8. In addressing public health matters, federal and state governments may choose to criminalize behavior or to subject it to a regulatory scheme, or both. If cloning is to be subject to governmental control, by what criteria would it decide what approach would be most effective?

9. While Congress has prohibited federal funding in many areas of reproductive technology and human embryo research, private research and much clinical practice proceeds without regulation. Unfortunately, this ban has resulted in an inability to monitor the state of research and safeguard the quality of clinical practice in the private arena. Does cloning present particular issues that require regulatory activity in the private sphere beyond the current voluntary moratorium? Should we develop an interdepartmental, federal body authorized to draft guidelines concerning cloning, and to evaluate whether any human cloning research or clinical applications should go forward?

10. Complex constitutional questions are raised by any congressional attempt to completely ban all human cloning. They include the extent of congressional power under the Commerce Clause, as well as First and Fourteenth Amendment issues. Although Congress can clearly deny federal funding to cloning research under its spending power, what is the extent of its power to regulate cloning in the private arena?

11. The United States operates within a global economy. Dr. Wilmut already has patented his technique for its commercial potential. Any solution the United States adopts regarding adult cloning must be international in perspective. What mechanisms and models are present to work toward an international consensus on issues related to adult cloning? What can the United States learn from the regulation of reproductive and genetic technologies in other countries?

EMBRYO CLONING: THE POINT

Richard A. McCormick

Richard A. McCormick, S.J., was teaching theology at the University of Notre Dame when he wrote the following article.

■ POINTS TO CONSIDER

1. Who was Dr. Jerry Hall, and what did he do?

2. How will one's approach to cloning vary?

3. Explain the practice of "eugenics" described by the author.

4. What influence would this practice of "eugenics" have on individuality?

5. What is the pre-implanted embryo? Why is it described as human life?

6. Summarize the author's uncertainty as to the human condition.

Richard A. McCormick, S.J., "Should We Clone Humans?" **The Christian Century**, November 17-24, 1993: 1148-1149. Copyright 1993, Christian Century Foundation. Reprinted by permission from the November 17-24, 1993, issue of **The Christian Century**.

We are increasingly encouraged to regard the human person simply as genetic data.

The cloning of human embryos by Dr. Jerry L. Hall at George Washington University Medical Center has set off an interesting ethical debate. Should it be done? For what purposes? With what controls? It is not surprising – though I find it appalling – that some commentators see the entire issue in terms of individual autonomy. Embryos belong to their producers, they argue, and it is not society's business to interfere with the exercise of people's privacy (see comments in the *New York Times,* October 26).

One's approach to cloning will vary according to the range of issues one wants to consider. For example, some people will focus solely on the role of cloning in aiding infertile couples – and they will likely conclude that there is nothing wrong with it. The scarcely hidden assumption is that anything that helps overcome infertility is morally appropriate. That is, I believe, frighteningly myopic.

Human cloning is an extremely social matter, not a question of mere personal privacy. I see three dimensions to the moral question: the wholeness of life, the individuality of life, and respect for life.

WHOLENESS

Our society has gone a long way down the road of positive eugenics, the preferential breeding of superior genotypes. People offhandedly refer to the "right to a healthy child." Implied in such loose talk is the right to discard the imperfect. What is meant, of course, is that couples have a claim to reasonably available means to ensure that their children are born healthy. We have pre-implementation diagnosis for genetics defects. We have recently seen several cases of "wrongful life" where the child herself or himself is the plaintiff. As a member of the ethics committee of the American Fertility Society, I regularly receive brochures from sperm banks stating the donor's race, education, hobbies, height, weight and eye color. We are rapidly becoming a pick-and-choose society with regard to our prospective children. More than a few couples withhold acceptance of their fetuses pending further testing.

This practice of eugenics raises a host of problems: What qualities are to be maximized? What defects are intolerable? Who decides? But the critical flaw in "preferential breeding" is the perversion of our attitudes: we begin to value the person in terms of the particular trait he or she was programmed to have. In short, we reduce the whole to a part. People who do that are in a moral wilderness.

INDIVIDUALITY

Uniqueness and diversity (sexual, racial, ethnic, cultural) are treasured aspects of the human condition, as was sharply noted by a study group of the National Council of Churches in 1984 (Genetic Engineering: Social and Ethical Consequences). Viewed theologically, human beings, in their enchanting, irreplaceable uniqueness and with all their differences, are made in the image of God. Eugenics schemes that would bypass, downplay or flatten human diversities and uniqueness should be viewed with a beady eye. In the age of the Genome Project, it is increasingly possible to collapse the human person into genetic data. Such reductionism could shatter our wonder at human individuality and diversity at the very time that, in other spheres of life, we are emphasizing it.

LIFE

Everyone admits that the pre-embryo (pre-implanted embryo) is human life. It is living, not dead. It is human, not canine. One need not attribute personhood to such early life to claim that it demands respect and protection.

Two considerations must be carefully weighed as we try to discern our obligations toward pre-embryonic life. The first consideration is for the potential of the pre-embryo. Under favorable circumstances, the fertilized ovum will move through developmental individuality and then progressively through functional, behavioral, psychic and social individuality. In viewing the first stage, one cannot afford to blot out subsequent stages. It retains its potential for personhood and thus deserves profound respect. This is a weighty matter for the believer who sees the human person as a member of God's family and the temple of the Spirit. Interference with such a potential future cannot be a light undertaking.

The second consideration concerns our own human condition. I would gather these concerns under the notion of "uncertainty." There is uncertainty about the extent to which enthusiasm for

Reprinted with permission from the **Star Tribune,** Minneapolis.

human research can be controlled. That is, if we concluded that pre-embryos need not be treated in all circumstances as persons, would we little by little extend this to embryos? These are not abstract worries; they have become live questions.

Furthermore, there is uncertainty about the effect of pre-embryo manipulation on personal and societal attitudes toward human life in general. Will there be further erosion of our respect? I say "further" because of the widespread acceptance and practice of abortion. There is grave uncertainty about our ability to say no and backtrack when we detect abuses, especially if they have produced valuable scientific and therapeutic data or significant treatment. Medical technology ("progress") has a way of establishing irreversible dynamics.

CONCLUSION

Because the pre-embryo does have intrinsic potential and because of the many uncertainties noted above, I would argue that the pre-embryo should be treated as a person. These obligations may be subject to qualifications. But when we are dealing with human life, the matter is too important to be left to local or regional criteria and controls. We need uniform national controls. Without them, our corporate reverence for life, already so deeply compromised, will be further eroded.

41

UNIFORMITY

There is biological as well as theological wisdom in the Apostle Paul's insight concerning the Church: It is good that the members are all different and that each has something special to contribute to the good of all.

Uniformity in the natural world is dangerous. Uniformity in the human race would be social disaster. If human cloning ever took hold on a large scale, would our humanity be limited by fads and fashions of a particular era?

Phil Wogaman, "Cloning: The Theological Implications," **Christian Social Action**, May, 1997, p. 35.

In sum, human cloning is not just another technological step to be judged in terms of its effects on those cloned. What frightens me above all is what human cloning would do to all of us – to our sense of the wholeness, individuality and sanctity of human life. These are intertwined theological concerns of the first magnitude.

READING

6

EMBRYO CLONING: THE COUNTERPOINT

Human Embryo Research Panel

The Human Embryo Research Panel issued a report to the nation dealing with the moral and political issues associated with scientific embryo research and cloning. The panel was established by the National Institutes of Health.

■ **POINTS TO CONSIDER**

1. How do extreme conservatives view the embryo?

2. Why would it be pointless and expensive to program people through cloning?

3. What did ethicists Singer and Wells say about embryo cloning?

4. Summarize arguments of those who favor cloning.

5. Do you support embryo cloning under any circumstances?

Excerpted from a report commissioned for the National Institutes of Health titled, "Human Embryo Research Panel: Volume II," September, 1994.

The fact that cloned individuals are likely to resemble each other, as twins do, does not seem to raise unique or especially troubling ethical problems.

The George Washington researchers took 17 embryos, at the two-to-eight cell stage, obtained from women undergoing in vitro fertilization (IVF) treatment. After separating the individual embryonic cells, called blastomeres, Jerry Hall and his colleagues placed the blastomeres in nutrient solutions where they could begin dividing again. The result was 48 new embryos, an average of three for each original embryo.

CONSERVATIVE POSITION

On the most extreme conservative position, the embryo is a human person, and must not be used in any nontherapeutic experimentation. However, few opponents of cloning espouse the conservative conception of the moral status of the embryo. They are not opposed to embryo research in itself, but rather specifically to cloning embryos. It may be that the term "cloning" is itself partly responsible for the opposition. The idea of cloning in the popular mind is of an evil dictator attempting to populate the world with his replicas, or hundreds of thousands of mindless individuals created by mad scientists to perform various tasks. However, as Singer and Wells point out, "If some mad dictator wished to program groups of people, it would be a pointless and expensive exercise to have them cloned first. Identical twins are not more susceptible to brainwashing techniques than single births, and no more would cloned individuals be."

Singer and Wells maintain that it is important to distinguish between cloning done for the purpose of producing living human beings and work that has no such intention. The most powerful reasons for cloning are to enable embryos to be genetically typed and to provide compatible tissues and organs for medical purposes. Moreover, the objections are weakest when directed against these forms of cloning. Since neither leads to a living human being, we can disregard objections based on the risk of an abnormal child or on the psychological problems that might face a cloned person.

This kind of cloning could not have led to the birth of a child, and hence any objections about the risk of physical or emotional problems of such a child do not apply. The researchers chose for

their experiment embryos with a fatal defect: they were formed from eggs fertilized by more than one sperm, giving them three or more set of chromosomes instead of two. Such embryos cannot be implanted and are certain to die. The longest-lasting embryos in the Hall-Stillman experiment survived only a few days to the 32-cell stage. Hall said, "We used these triploid embryos so as not to get into an ethical debate." The inability of the embryos to survive more than a few days was important in getting the approval of the hospital's ethics committee. According to the head of the committee, Gail Povar, "What we're talking about here is nonviable human chromosomal tissue. I don't consider this to be human cloning. I consider it the manipulation of pathological specimens."

IN SUPPORT OF CLONING

Not everyone opposes cloning human embryos for transplantation. Andrea Bonnicksen writes, "If embryo biopsy is shown to be safe, a logical extension of the technique will be to "twin" an embryo, as is already done in animal husbandry, and create a "duplicate" embryo to be preserved and transferred to the women in the event the first embryo fails to implant." From this perspective, cloning is simply another method for obtaining more embryos for implantation in in vitro fertilization (IVF), no different from extracting and fertilizing eggs. Moreover, it has the advantage of not inducing superovulation in women, with all of its attendant risks, in order to extract a sufficient number of eggs. Embryo cloning is a way to produce multiple embryos without the cost, side effects, or possible risks associated with hormone treatment.

45

Given these advantages, why the opposition to cloning? The objection seems to be that it could lead to "Brave New World" scenarios. For example, parents might be able to save identical copies of embryos so that, if their child ever needed an organ transplant, the mother could give birth to the child's identical twin, a perfect match for organ donation.

Would this be morally wrong? Something analogous was done a few years ago by the Ayala family, when Mary Ayala conceived a child specifically to be a bone marrow donor to her older sister, Anissa, who was dying of leukemia. The reaction from medical ethicists was generally negative; the Ayalas were seen as treating the new baby as a "mere means," contrary to basic ethics. However, it can be argued that conceiving a baby to serve as a donor is not necessarily treating her as a mere means, so long as her family will love her as a person in her own right once she is born, and the donation does not impose unacceptable risks on her. If Anissa already had a baby sister with compatible bone marrow, her parents could undoubtedly ask the doctors to do the transplant to save Anissa's life. Why should the moral situation be different if their choice is to try and conceive a sibling with compatible marrow?

OTHER WORRIES

Another worry is that parents might store cloned embryos as replacement children. For example, they could keep a frozen embryo as a backup in case their child died, so they could create the perfect replacement. However, parents who store an extra embryo for this purpose are likely to be sorely disappointed. Even though the two embryos would be genetically identical, the resulting children would not be. The reason is that cytoplasm plays a role in directing gene expression, and so cells created by nuclear transplantation are never identical to the donor because of this cytoplasmic difference. Moreover, the embryonic environment has large influences on the development of the embryo. Consequently, genetically identical embryos allowed to develop in the same mother at different times would not turn out to be identical. Environmental differences also come into play. That is why identical twins, gestated at the same time, never have identical personalities and often do not look exactly alike either.

The same response can be given to the objection raised by Dr. Arthur Caplan, that cloning is "morally suspect" because it allows

46

us to know what someone will be like in the future. For example, twins that become twins separated by years or decades let us see things about our future that we don't want to. You may not want to know, at 40, what you will look like at 60. And parents should not be looking at a baby and seeing the infant 20 years later in an older sibling...Is that fair to the child? What expectations will you put on them?

Relatives often do resemble each other (which is why it used to be said, in a more sexist age, that before marrying a woman, a man should take a good look at her mother). The fact that cloned individuals are likely to closely resemble each other, as twins do, does not seem to raise unique or especially troubling ethical problems. Twins are not exact replicas of each other, and so cloning does not let us see our futures, even if that were thought to be a very bad thing.

It is not clear why parents who have conceived using IVF should expect that they have created a perfect child, any more than parents who conceive in the ordinary way. In any event, as already noted, they should not expect the cloned embryo to be a replica of the first child. It is not possible to duplicate a child. It should not be assumed that there is no scientific value in cloning embryos because the idea makes some people uncomfortable.

READING

7

CLONING SHOULD NOT BE BANNED

John A. Robertson

John A. Robertson, J.D., is the Vinson and Elkins Chair in Law at the University of Texas School of Law in Austin, Texas.

■ POINTS TO CONSIDER

1. Why does cloning seem offensive and dangerous?

2. Identify the beneficial uses of cloning.

3. Summarize the unsubstantiated harms from cloning.

4. Discuss the most important fears about cloning.

5. How does cloning differ from other reproductive technology?

Excerpted from testimony by John A. Robertson before the Subcommittee on Public Health and Safety of the Senate Committee on Labor and Human Resources, June 17, 1997.

*There is a real danger that prohibitions on cloning
will open the door to inappropriate restrictions on
accepted medical and genetic practices.*

The prospect of human cloning raises important ethical, legal, and social issues that need careful attention. An essential part of that debate is the recognition that cloning could serve important reproductive needs, just as current practices of assisted reproduction and genetic selection do. Yet cloning differs from those practices in certain ways. The debate over cloning should thus focus on whether cloning poses such additional risks of harm over existing practices to justify different legal or policy treatment. My own opinion is that it does not, but I acknowledge that much more thought, debate, and analysis is needed before we are ready to determine public policy for human cloning.

In the abstract the idea of cloning humans does seem offensive and dangerous. It is easy to imagine horrific scenarios of power-hungry dictators cloning a subject class, or narcissistic tycoons creating multiples of themselves. A closer, more considered look, however, reveals that the most likely uses of human cloning would be by married couples who are infertile or at risk for severe genetic disease, who want to rear healthy, biologically-related children.

LEGITIMATE, BENEFICIAL USES OF CLONING

Rearing healthy, biologically-related children is the source of great meaning in our lives. The freedom to do so undergirds our constitutional rights of procreative liberty and drives current medical practices in assisted reproduction and prenatal screening. Because having and rearing children is such a central part of our personal freedom, government should not ban practices necessary to achieve that goal unless it can be shown that tangible harm to others would result from the reproductive or selection technique in question.

The debate over human cloning has given too little attention to ways in which human cloning could legitimately be used to enable infertile and genetically at risk couples to rear biologically-related children in a loving family environment, just as mainstream techniques of assisted reproduction and prenatal genetic selection do. Cloning aids that enterprise in two significant ways.

EMBRYOS

First, cloning embryos created in the process of in vitro fertilization (IVF) treatment of infertility could increase the supply of embryos available for implantation, without requiring that women undergo the significant physical burdens and expense of additional cycles of ovarian stimulation and surgical retrieval of eggs.

Second, somatic cell cloning would enable a married couple that is infertile due to egg or sperm deficiencies to use their own DNA to produce a child, thus avoiding the risks and impersonality of purchasing sperm or eggs from commercial sperm banks or anonymous egg donors. This would also assure the child a genetic link with the rearing partner who lacks viable gametes (as now occurs in sperm or egg but not in embryo donation), and a biological tie through gestation with the other. Understood in this context, cloning is not radically or essentially different from many current medical and genetic practices.

CLONING DIFFERS

Cloning, nevertheless, does differ in some ways from existing reproductive and selection technology. It actively seeks to replicate DNA and selects or replicates the entire genome (except for mitochondria). While cloning could lead to some unique relational and rearing situations, it offers advantages over current practices with unknown and genetically-unrelated sperm, egg, and embryo donors. The ethical issues raised by cloning are thus not qualitatively different from the ethical issues that arise in current assisted reproduction and genetic selection practices. If cloning does not lead to tangible harm to others (as I argue below that it does not), it should be no less legally available to infertile couples than are other techniques of treating infertility and assuring healthy children. Indeed, it is difficult to explain why cloning as a way of forming a healthy family is wrong and should be made criminal, but these other practices, to which cloning is closely related, are not. There is a real danger that prohibitions on cloning will open the door to inappropriate restrictions on accepted medical and genetic practices.

"...WELL THAT MOVIE MADE UP MY MIND... I'M AGAINST HUMAN CLONING!..."

UNSUBSTANTIATED HARMS FROM HUMAN CLONING

Given the potential benefits of human cloning to infertile and genetically at risk couples, a ban on its use should not be enacted unless human cloning would lead to clear, substantial harm to others. But the case for harm to children or others in the reproductive settings that I have mentioned is very difficult to show, and does not meet the high threshold of harm necessary to justify federal restrictions on family and reproductive decisions.

A frequently voiced objection to human cloning is that it violates the essence of being human because a person is conceived asexually in the laboratory rather than sexually in love-making. That view, however, is not the only reasonable conception of the essence of our humanity. There are many others. Some are based on religious views, others on one's personal philosophy. An equally cogent view locates the essence of humanity in consciousness and the ability to think and feel – a state perfectly consistent with human cloning. Appeals to particularistic, personal views of the essence of humanity are simply too weak a basis to support criminal bans on reproductive practices, just as they are insufficient to ban heart transplants from brain-dead cadavers to patients with end-stage cardiac disease.

IMPORTANT FEARS

The most important fears about cloning are based on the welfare of resulting children. The National Bioethics Advisory Commission had one aspect of this concern in mind when it cited safety considerations as a justification at the present time for a federal ban on human cloning. It is highly unlikely, however, that clinical uses of human cloning would occur without extensive animal research that first established its safety and efficacy. Couples interested in using cloning to form a family would have little interest in a technique that led to physical defects in children.

A second aspect about the resulting child's welfare concerns its rights and status. In the most likely cloning scenario, parents will be seeking to rear a biologically-related or chosen child whom they will love for itself. But even in less benign situations, any resulting child would be a person with all the moral and legal rights of persons, and no more would be the property or subject of the person who commissions or carries out the cloning than any other child.

A third aspect about the child's welfare are fears that a child's autonomy and individuality will be reduced because it will have the same DNA as another person, either living or dead. But the child who results from cloning will not be the same person as the clone source, even if the two share many physical characteristics. Its uterine, early childhood, and overall rearing environment and experiences will be different. Given the importance of nurture in making us who we are, the danger that the person cloned will lack a unique individuality is highly fanciful.

PERSONAL IDENTITY

But even if genetic replication does not totally control personal identity, the genes chosen are likely to have some effect on who the person is. After all, DNA that is cloned was chosen precisely because it had significance for the commissioning couple. The fear here is that rearing parents will have rigid or unrealistic expectations about the child precisely because of the genome chosen. They could end up disappointed in the child, or embark on a socialization or rearing process to shape the child according to its genes, thus denying the child its own autonomy and individuality.

The ethical claim here is that cloning, even in the medically legitimate scenarios that I have sketched, robs the child of an open future. But there is no basis for thinking that children whose DNA has been chosen will be any more endangered by unrealistic parental expectations than other children who are deeply invested with parental hopes and desires. Nor is their future any less open because they have the same DNA as a living or dead person. The fact that we can glimpse something of our future by looking at persons with similar genes doesn't prevent us from making and choosing our futures as we live our lives.

This is not to deny that cloning scenarios in which married couples rear a child that has the DNA of one of them, of a previously existing child, or of a third party may present some unique psychological problems. But these problems do not appear substantially or qualitatively different from similar problems that arise from the use of frozen embryos, sperm, egg, and embryo donors, and the genetic selection that now occurs at preconception and prenatal stages of reproduction. Nor are they so serious or threatening that they could be said to make the very life of a cloned child – who would not otherwise exist but for the cloning in question – so full of suffering or confused identity that any existence as a clone is less preferable than nonexistence.

A BAN ON HUMAN CLONING IS UNWISE AND UNJUSTIFIED

At this early stage in the development of cloning, it is essential to continue the debate about potential uses and harms of cloning, and not hastily enact legislation. Fortunately, we have time to assess and ponder these issues, because the possibility of clinical applications of cloning to humans is still some time away.

In such a situation of ongoing debate, Congress should be very slow to restrict familial uses of cloning, because they are so intimately involved with personal decisions about family and reproduction. A federal criminal prohibition on human cloning risks depriving infertile couples of a potentially legitimate way of forming families, threatens established practices in reproductive medicine and genetic screening, and would establish a dangerous precedent for federal intervention in family and reproductive matters. Nothing that we know about how human cloning is likely to be used justifies such a step.

READING

8

THE NECESSITY OF A PERMANENT BAN

Leon Kass

Dr. Leon Kass teaches bioethics at the University of Chicago. He has been concerned with the issue of cloning for many years. Cloning was the topic of his first paper on bioethics over 25 years ago.

■ POINTS TO CONSIDER

1. Identify the radical truth about human cloning.

2. Why are there no compelling reasons for human cloning?

3. Summarize the four principal objections to human cloning given by the author.

4. How would cloning be a step toward manufacturing people?

5. Explain how cloning would disrupt the parent-child relationship.

Excerpted from testimony by Leon Kass before the National Bioethics Advisory Committee, March 14, 1997.

We would be taking a major step into making man himself simply another one of the man-made things.

BIOETHICS 25 YEARS AGO

We have in some sense been softened up to the idea of human cloning through movies, cartoons, jokes and intermittent commentary in the media. We have also become accustomed to new practices in human reproduction, in vitro fertilization, embryo manipulation and surrogate pregnancy, and in animal biotechnology, the transgenic animal science and a burgeoning science of genetic engineering.

Changes in the broader culture now make it more difficult to express a common respectful understanding of sexuality, procreation, life and the meaning of motherhood, fatherhood and the links between the generations. In a world whose once given natural boundaries are blurred by technological change and whose moral boundaries are seemingly up for grabs, it is much more difficult to make the compelling case against human cloning.

Therefore, the first thing of which I want to persuade you is not to be complacent about what is here at issue. Human cloning, though in some respects continuous with previous reproductive technologies, also represents something radically new, both in itself and in its easily foreseeable consequences.

A RADICAL TRUTH

The stakes here are very high, indeed. Let me exaggerate but in the direction of the truth. You have been asked to give advice on nothing less than whether human procreation is going to remain human, whether children are going to be made rather than begotten, and whether it is a good thing humanly speaking to say "yes" to the road which leads at best to the dehumanized rationality of the brave new world.

If I could persuade you of nothing else it would be this: What we have here is not business as usual to be fretted about and given our seal of approval. Please rise to the occasion and advise as if the future of our humanity may, indeed, hang in the balance.

Offensive, grotesque, revolting, repugnant, repulsive. These are the words most commonly heard these days regarding the prospect of human cloning. Such reactions one hears from both the man or woman in the street and from the intellectuals, from believers and atheists, from humanists and scientists. Even Dolly's creator, Dr. Wilmut, has said that he would "find it offensive to clone a human being." People are repelled by many aspects of human cloning.

NO REASONS

Almost no one sees any compelling reason for human cloning. Almost everyone anticipates its possible misuses and abuses. Many feel oppressed by the sense that there is nothing we can do to prevent it from happening, and this makes the prospect seem all the more revolting. Revulsion is surely not an argument. Some of yesterday's repugnancies are today calmly accepted. But I submit in crucial cases repugnance is often the emotional bearer of deep wisdom beyond reason's power to articulate it fully.

Can anyone really give an argument adequate to the horror which is father-daughter incest even under consent or having sex with animals or eating human flesh, or even just raping or murdering another human being? Would anyone's failure to give full rational justification for his revulsion at these practices make that revulsion ethically suspect? Not at all. In my view our repugnance at human cloning belongs in this category. We are repelled by the prospect of cloning human beings, not because of the strangeness or novelty of the undertaking, but because we feel immediately and without argument the violation of things we rightfully hold dear.

FOUR OBJECTIONS

I doubt very much whether I can give proper rational voice to this horror, but in the remarks that follow I will try. Also consider seriously that this may be one of those instances about which the heart has its reasons that reason cannot adequately know.

I will raise four kinds of objections: the ethics of experimentation, identity and individuality, fabrication and manufacture, despotism and the violation of what it means to have children. *First,* any attempt to clone a human being would constitute an unethical experiment upon the resulting child to be. As the animal experiments indicate, there is grave risk of mishaps and deformities. Moreover, one cannot presume a future cloned child's consent to be a clone, even a healthy one. Thus, I submit again we cannot ethically get to know even whether or not human cloning is feasible.

I understand, of course, that it is philosophically impossible to compare life with defects against nonexistence, but that problem aside, it is surely true that people can harm and even maim children in the very act of conceiving them, say by paternal transmission of the HIV virus or maternal transmission of heroin dependence. To do so intentionally or even negligently is inexcusable and clearly unethical.

Second, cloning creates serious issues of identity and individuality. The cloned person may experience concerns about his distinctive identity, because he will be in genotype and appearance identical to another human being; but in this case, it will be to a twin who might be his father or mother. What would be the psychic burdens of being the child or parent of your twin? Moreover, the cloned individual will be saddled with a genotype that has already lived. He will not be fully a surprise to the world, and people are likely always to compare his performances in life with that of his alter ego.

Genetic distinctiveness symbolizes the uniqueness of each human life and the independence of its parents that each human child rightfully attains. It can also be an important support for living a worthy and dignified life. Such arguments apply with great force to any large scale replication of human individuals. They are in my view sufficient to rebut even the first attempts to clone a human being. One must never forget that these are human beings upon whom our eugenic or merely playful fantasies are to be enacted.

MANUFACTURING

Third, human cloning would represent a giant step towards turning begetting into making, and procreation into manufacture, a process already begun with in vitro fertilization and genetic testing of embryos. With cloning, the total genetic blueprint of the cloned individual is selected and determined by the human artisans. To be sure, subsequent development is still according to natural processes, and the resulting children will still be recognizably human. But we here would be taking a major step into making man himself simply another one of the man-made things. Human nature becomes merely the last part of nature to succumb to the technological project. This project turns all of nature into raw material at human disposal to be governed by our rationalized technique, but only according to the prevailing subjective prejudices of the moment.

Scientists who clone animals make it perfectly clear that they are engaged in instrument making. The animals are from the start designed as means to serve rational human purpose. In human cloning scientists and perspective parents would be adapting the same technocratic mentality to human children. Human children would be their artifacts even if they loved them. Such an arrangement is profoundly dehumanizing no matter how good the product. Mass scale cloning of the same individual makes the point vividly. But the violation of human equality, freedom and dignity is present even in a single planned clone.

PROCREATION

Finally and perhaps most important, the practice of human cloning by nuclear transfer, like other anticipated forms of genetic engineering of the next generation, would enshrine and aggravate a profound and mischief-making misunderstanding of the meaning of having children and of the parent-child relationship. When a couple now chooses to procreate, the partners are saying "yes" to the emergence of new life in its novelty, are saying "yes" not only to having a child, but also tacitly to having whatever child this child turns out to be. Whether we know it or not, we are thereby also saying "yes" to our mortality, to the necessity of our replacement, and the limits of our control.

In this way of nature to say yes to the future by procreating means precisely that we are relinquishing our grip even as we thereby take up our own share in what we hope will be the immortality of human life and the human species. This means that our children are not our children. They are not our property. They are not our possessions. Neither are they supposed to live our lives for us or anyone else's life but their own.

To be sure, we seek to guide them on their way, imparting to them not just life but nurture, love and a way of life. To be sure, they bear our hopes that they will surpass us in goodness and happiness, enabling us in small measure to transcend our own limitations. But their genetic distinctiveness and independence is the natural foreshadowing of the deep truth that they have their own and never-before-enacted life to live. Though sprung from a past they take an unchartered course into the future.

Much mischief is already done by parents who try to live vicariously through their children. Children are sometimes compelled to fulfill the broken dreams of unhappy parents. John Doe, Jr., or the III, is under the burden of having to live up to his forbearer's name. But in cloning such overbearing parents take at the start a decisive step which contradicts the entire meaning of the open and forward-looking nature of parent-child relations. The child is given a genotype that has already lived with full expectation that this blueprint of a past life ought to be controlling of a life that is to come.

Cloning is thus inherently despotic for it seeks to make one's children or someone else's children after one's own image or an image of one's choosing and their future according to one's will. In some cases the despotism may be mild and benevolent and in others mischievous and downright tyrannical. But despotism, the control of another through one's own will, it will unavoidably be.

CONCLUSION

What then should we do? We should declare human cloning, that is the attempt to create a human person by nuclear transfer, deeply unethical in itself and dangerous in its likely consequences. In so doing we shall have the backing of the overwhelming majority, not only of our fellow Americans but of the human race, including, I believe, most practicing scientists.

Next we should do all that we can to prevent human cloning in this limited sense from happening by an international legal ban if possible, by a unilateral national ban at a minimum. Scientists can, of course, secretly undertake to violate such a law, but they will at least be deterred by not being able to stand up proudly to claim the credit for their technological bravado and success.

Such a ban on human cloning will not harm the progress of basic genetic embryological science and technology. On the contrary, it will reassure the public that scientists are happy to proceed without violating the deep ethical norms and institutions of the human community.

READING

9

A DECLARATION IN DEFENSE OF CLONING

International Academy of Humanism

The signers of the following Declaration are Humanist Laureates of the International Academy of Humanism.

■ POINTS TO CONSIDER

1. What service has science performed for humans in the past century?

2. How should any guidelines restricting cloning be written?

3. Define the moral issues raised by cloning.

4. Discuss the way spiritual agendas may influence decisions society may make about restricting human cloning.

5. Why are the signers of this Declaration in favor of cloning?

"Declaration in Defense of Cloning and the Integrity of Scientific Research," **Free Inquiry**, Summer, 1997: 11-12.

Humankind's rich repertoire of thoughts, feelings, aspirations, and hopes seems to arise from electro-chemical brain processes, not from an immaterial soul that operates in ways no instrument can discover.

We, the undersigned, welcome announcements of major advances in the cloning of higher animals. Throughout this century, the physical, biological, and behavioral sciences have placed important new capabilities within human reach. On balance, these advances have contributed to enormous improvements in human welfare. Where novel technologies have raised legitimate ethical questions, the human community has in general demonstrated its willingness to confront those questions openly and to seek answers that enhance the general welfare.

The cloning of higher animals raises ethical concerns. Appropriate guidelines need to be developed that will prevent abuses, while making the benefits of cloning maximally available. Such guidelines should respect to the greatest extent possible the autonomy and choice of each individual human being. Every effort should be made not to block the freedom and integrity of scientific research.

HUMAN CLONING

No one has demonstrated a present capability to clone humans. Yet the very possibility that contemporary achievements may open a path toward cloning has sparked a hail of protests. We view with concern the widespread calls to delay, defund, or discontinue cloning research which have come from sources as disparate as President Bill Clinton in the United States, President Jacques Chirac of France, former Prime Minister John Major of Great Britain, and the Vatican in Rome.

We believe that reason is humanity's most powerful tool for managing the problems that it encounters. But reasoned argument has been a scarce commodity in the recent flood of attacks on cloning. Critics have delighted in drawing parallels to Mary Shelley's Frankenstein, predicting terrible consequences if researchers dare to press on with questions whose answers "man was not meant to know." Behind the critiques seems to lie the assumption that human cloning would raise moral issues more profound than those faced in connection with any previous scientific or technological development.

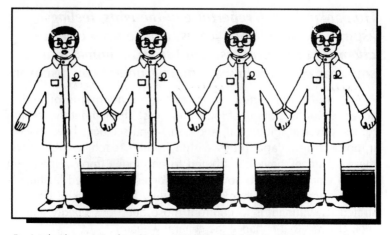

MORAL ISSUES

What moral issues would human cloning raise? Some religions teach that human beings are fundamentally different from other mammals – that humans have been imbued with immortal souls by a deity, giving them a value which cannot be compared to that of other living things. Human nature is held to be unique and sacred. Scientific advances that pose a perceived risk of altering this "nature" are angrily opposed.

Deeply rooted as such ideas may be in dogma, we question whether these should be used to decide whether human beings will be permitted to benefit from new biotechnology. As far as the scientific enterprise can determine, *Homo sapiens* is a member of the animal kingdom. Human capabilities appear to differ in degree, not in kind, from those found among the higher animals. Humankind's rich repertoire of thoughts, feelings, aspirations, and hopes seems to arise from electrochemical brain processes, not from an immaterial soul that operates in ways no instrument can discover.

SPIRITUAL AGENDAS

The immediate question raised by the current debate over cloning is, therefore, do advocates of supernatural or spiritual agendas have truly meaningful qualifications to contribute to that debate? Surely everyone has the right to be heard. But we believe that there is a very real danger that research with enormous potential benefits may be suppressed solely because it conflicts with some people's religious beliefs. It is important to recognize that similar religious objections were once raised against autopsies, anesthesia, artificial insemination, and the entire genetic revolution of our day – yet enormous benefits have accrued from each of these developments. A view of human nature rooted in humanity's mythical past ought not to be our primary criterion for making moral decisions about cloning.

We see no inherent ethical dilemmas in cloning nonhuman higher animals. Nor is it clear to us that future developments in cloning human tissues or even cloning human beings will create moral predicaments beyond the capacity of human reason to resolve. The moral issues raised by cloning are neither larger nor more profound than the questions human beings have already faced in regards to such technologies as nuclear energy, recombinant DNA, and computer encryption. They are simply new.

THE LUDDITES

Historically, the Luddite option, which seeks to turn back the clock and limit or prohibit the application of already existing technologies, has never proven realistic or productive. The potential benefits of cloning may be so immense that it would be a tragedy if ancient theological scruples should lead to a Luddite rejection of cloning. We call for continued, responsible development of cloning technologies, and for a broad-based commitment to ensuring that traditionalist views do not obstruct beneficial scientific developments.

The signers of the Declaration are Humanist Laureates of the International Academy of Humanism:

Pieter Admiraal, Medical Doctor, The Netherlands

Ruben Ardila, psychologist, National University of Colombia, Colombia

Sir Isaiah Berlin, Professor Emeritus of Philosophy, Oxford University, U.K.

Sir Hermann Bondi, Fellow of the Royal Society, Past Master, Churchill College, Cambridge University, U.K.

Vern Bullough, Visiting Professor of Nursing, California State University at Northridge, U.S.A.

Mario Bunge, Professor of Philosophy of Science, McGill University, Canada

Bernard Crick, Professor Emeritus of Politics, Birkbeck College, University of London, U.K.

Francis Crick, Nobel Laureate in Physiology, Salk Institute, U.S.A.

Richard Dawkins, Charles Simionyi Professor of Public Understanding of Science, Oxford University, U.K.

José Delgado, Director, Centro de Estudios Neurobiologicos,Spain

Paul Edwards, Professor of Philosophy, New School for Social Research, U.S.A.

Antony Flew, Professor Emeritus of Philosophy, Reading University, U.K.

Johan Galtung, Professor of Sociology, University of Oslo, Norway

Adolf Grünbaum, Professor of Philosophy, University of Pittsburgh, U.S.A.

Herbert Hauptman, Nobel Laureate, Professor of Biophysical Science, State University of New York at Buffalo, U.S.A.

Alberto Hidalgo Tuñón, President, Sociedad Asturiana de Filosofía, Spain

Sergei Kapitza, Chair, Moscow Institute of Physics and Technology, Russia

Paul Kurtz, Professor Emeritus of Philosophy, State University of New York at Buffalo, U.S.A.

Gerald A. Larue, Professor Emeritus of Archeology and Biblical Studies, University of Southern California at Los Angeles, U.S.A.

Thelma Z. Lavine, Professor of Philosophy, George Mason University, U.S.A.

Jose Leite Lopes, Director, Centro Brasiliero de Pesquisas Fisicas, Brazil

Taslima Nasrin, Author, Physician, Social Critic, Bangladesh

Indumati Parikh, Reformer and Activist, India

Jean-Claude Pecker, Professor Emeritus of Astrophysics, College de France, Academy of Sciences, France

W.V. Quine, Professor Emeritus of Philosophy, Harvard University, U.S.A.

J.J.C. Smart, Professor of Philosophy, University of Adelaide, Australia

V.M. Tarkunde, Reformer and Activist, India

Richard Taylor, Professor Emeritus of Philosophy, University of Rochester, U.S.A.

Simone Veil, Former President, European Parliament, France

Kurt Vonnegut, Novelist, U.S.A.

Edward O. Wilson, Professor Emeritus of Sociobiology, Harvard University, U.S.A.

A DECLARATION IN OPPOSITION

Edmund D. Pellegrino

Edmund D. Pellegrino, M.D., is the John Carroll Professor of Medicine and Medical Ethics at Georgetown University in Washington, D.C.

■ POINTS TO CONSIDER

1. What kind of cloning ban was proposed by the National Commission on Bioethics?

2. Why does the author disagree with this proposal?

3. How are human embryos defined by the author?

4. Why is the author opposed to cloning?

Excerpted from testimony by Edmund D. Pellegrino before the Subcommittee on Public Health and Safety of the Senate Committee on Labor and Human Resources, June 17, 1997.

Their reasons for recommending a ban are morally sound.

President Clinton and his National Commission on Bioethics have recently announced that human cloning by the technique of somatic cell nuclear transfer is morally wrong, and should be banned because of its potential for grave physical and psychosocial harm both to the child and to fundamental family and social values American society cherishes. These harms they believe outweigh the benefits of human cloning in treating and preventing disease.

Their reasons for recommending a ban are morally sound as far as they go. They are consistent with the moral principles of respect for persons. Unfortunately, the President and his Commission propose a temporary ban of five years. This undercuts the moral probity of their recommendation for two reasons. First, it suggests that something inherently wrong can be in time made right, and second, it begs the question of the moral wrong of human embryo experimentation which is the first and essential step in any cloning of human beings. I will confine my remarks to these two moral inconsistencies, since they are likely to be at the heart of any discussion of the President's proposed Cloning Prohibition Act of 1997.

TEMPORARY BAN

The President and his Commission propose a temporary five year ban on cloning to gain time to study the nature and degrees of potential harms of cloning. They deem the procedure "not safe at this point" but would permit cloning of embryos so long as there is no intent to implant them in a woman's womb.

This assertion compounds two moral errors. First, it assumes that something grievously wrong can become morally right by extended discussion "before this technology can be used." This converts the grievous harms they now see into matters of preference and attitude, making moral truth the creature of public opinion and plebiscite. The moral harms of cloning are inherent in the concept itself, and in the fact that obtaining further information about harms and hazards depends upon the deliberate manufacture, manipulation, and destruction of human embryos.

Human embryos are members of the human species in its earliest and most vulnerable stages. When they are manufactured to answer questions of harm, they themselves are harmed and thus become experimental subjects created to serve the interests of others. The President's legislation prohibits manufacturing of embryos with intent to implant, but it does not forbid making embryos. Implicitly it invites their manufacture as a means of gathering information in the interim of the ban. Thousands of embryos will be deliberately created, manipulated, and destroyed. We must not forget that it took 277 attempts to make one sheep.

Embryo research recommended three years ago by a special National Institutes for Health (NIH) panel is presently under Presidential ban. Yet the Commission's report tacitly accepts the NIH panel's recommendation and gives it new life by suggesting that embryo research will be needed to resolve unanswered questions. This is a logically and morally inconsistent argument. To be consistent a permanent ban should be placed on human cloning, because it depends on a first step which is itself morally indefensible.

CONCLUSION

Cloning of DNA molecules or of individual human cells and tissues not taken from manufactured, cloned embryos is morally licit. The information obtained can be useful in diagnosing, treating, and preventing human genetic disorders without resort to cloning whole human beings.

A permanent ban on human cloning while morally correct will not prevent uses and abuses of this technique. Recently the *New York Times* reported that a person named Randolf Wicker has decided to seek a scientist to help him clone himself. Human narcissism and commercial advantage suggest that humans will be cloned. Legislation cannot assure that citizens will act morally. What it can do is restrain an inherently immoral practice, refuse social approval, and provide legal recourse for children harmed by those who seek to create new beings in their own images.

READING

11

ETHICAL COUNTERPOINTS ON HUMAN CLONING: AN OVERVIEW

Ezekiel J. Emanuel

Ezekiel J. Emanuel, M.D., Ph.D., is a member of the National Bioethics Advisory Commission. He is also a member of the Department of Medicine at the Harvard Medical School.

■ POINTS TO CONSIDER

1. Why do arguments in favor of human cloning usually appeal to the rights of people?

2. Why are arguments that appeal to social values hard to express?

3. Define the two main ethical arguments in favor of human cloning.

4. Identify the three main ethical arguments opposed to human cloning.

5. How do you stand on the issue of human cloning? Why?

Excerpted from testimony by Ezekiel J. Emanuel before the Subcommittee on Public Health and Safety of the Senate Committee on Labor and Human Resources, June 17, 1997.

Science is not amoral; it must be conducted within ethical limits.

Arguments in favor of cloning human beings generally appeal to the rights of people to control their reproduction and the rights of scientists to free inquiry. Ethical arguments made in the language of rights and interests are easily understood; they are the terms in which Americans usually present their ethical claims. Conversely, arguments against cloning human beings appeal to psychological harms and threats to social values necessary for children to flourish and the indirect harms that come when these important social values are undermined. The United States is so focused on individual rights that arguments appealing to social values and ideas about human flourishing are much harder to express. As the Harvard legal scholar Mary Ann Glendon has stated: "We can barely find the words to speak of indirect harms, cumulative injury, or damages that appear only long after the acts that precipitated them." But the difficulty in expressing them should not necessarily be construed as implying that they are weak ethical arguments.

THE ETHICAL ARGUMENTS IN FAVOR OF CLONING HUMAN BEINGS

There are two main arguments in favor of using somatic cell nuclear transfer technology to clone human beings. The *first* argument appeals to the right to reproductive liberty. Individual autonomy is a core American value. Our society believes individuals should be free to pursue their own life plans and ideas of personal fulfillment.

Personal choices about reproduction are an essential aspect of individual autonomy. Not only are choices about reproduction intensely personal, they are of critical importance to a person's identity and a meaningful and fulfilling life. Because of the central importance of reproduction to autonomy, American society recognizes a person's right to reproductive liberty, to not having the state interfere with individual reproductive choices. Thus, we recognize an individual's right not to reproduce through the use of contraceptives as well as the right to use reproductive technologies such as artificial insemination and in vitro fertilization.

Somatic cell nuclear transfer technology is simply another mechanism for reproduction. To respect autonomy and the right

to reproductive liberty, we should permit individuals to decide whether to bear a child using somatic cell nuclear transfer technology or not, just as they can decide whether to use in vitro fertilization or not.

While individual autonomy and the particular right to reproductive liberty are neither absolute nor unlimited, they are so fundamental that they can be limited only for compelling reasons, such as serious harm to third parties. Since there are no serious harms to third parties from cloning human beings, and what harms may exist are too speculative and unproven, cloning should be permitted.

Those opposed to cloning reject this analysis and argue that cloning is qualitatively different from other reproductive technologies and not encompassed by the right to reproductive liberty. Cloning is asexual; it does not involve an exchange of genes, participation by males and females, and, therefore, is more like replicating a copy of what exists than creating a new being from the contributions of two humans. Further, it is argued that what is claimed for in cloning is not a right to reproduce but a right to create a child with a specific genetic endowment. Cloning is less about the meaning and fulfillment of one's own life and more about controlling the nature and characteristics of another human being. Controlling others is not a right that should be respected; the good of the child also needs consideration.

73

The *second* main argument in favor of cloning human beings is the right to scientific inquiry. Freedom of scientific inquiry is an important value both intrinsically, for its own sake, and instrumentally, for the benefits it produces. But science is not amoral; it must be conducted within ethical limits. We have recognized this by the codes of conduct for biomedical research such as the Nuremberg Code and the Declaration of Helsinki. We also recognize clinical research must be conducted in accord with the norms of informed consent. Therefore, the right to scientific inquiry is not absolute; various experiments and techniques can be regulated not to limit knowledge, but to protect the well-being of individuals and other public interests. If the government deemed the harms from somatic cell nuclear transfer technology to be sufficiently compelling, scientific inquiry could be regulated and even restricted.

ETHICAL ARGUMENTS OPPOSED TO THE CLONING OF HUMAN BEINGS

The Commission divided ethical arguments against cloning of human beings into three types: those related to 1) physical harms, 2) psychological harms to the child, and 3) harms to shared social understandings and values.

First, those opposed to cloning of human beings contend that the scientific progress on somatic cell nuclear transfer technology is too immature, and the data suggests that cloning of human beings would be physically dangerous. We have had only one successful cloning of a mammalian somatic cell nucleus and hundreds of failures in sheep and other mammals, such as mice. Further, there are other potential risks about which we have limited information: 1) cumulative nuclear mutations that may lead to cancer, deformities, and other diseases in the offspring, 2) premature aging of the clone, and other potential risks to normal development.

Second, while advocates argue cloning would enhance the autonomy of parents, opponents worry that cloning would undermine the autonomy and individuality of children. Here the worry is about the internal experience of the children who would result from somatic cell nuclear transfer. The philosopher Hans Jonas has said that people have a right to be ignorant of their future, and ignorant of the effect of their genome on their character and choices. Joe Feinberg, a legal scholar, put it in terms of having a right to an "open future" and being able to construct one's own life without it being previously laid out. The worry is that having the identical genetic endowment as someone who has already existed would rob a cloned child of his "separateness." Cloned children would feel that their life is lived under a shadow, as if it has already been lived and played out by another; that one's fate is already determined, that one's choices would not really be free or one's own, but imitations of the person who lived before.

A *third* worry raised by opponents is that cloning will undermine a complex web of social understandings and values at the heart of cherishing children. One effect of cloning may be for parents and society to view children as objects and things. When we speak of using people as things we generally have in mind two distinct actions. First, the person is made to serve someone else's goal or purpose; the person is used as a means to my ends and aims rather than his or her own ends. The person becomes the object of someone else's will. Second, the person ceases to be valued intrinsically, but the person's worth is determined by whether he or she possesses certain desirable characteristics. We evaluate the person like material things, like a car and computers, by whether they have certain characteristics and meet specific performance standards.

Unlike genetic screening that is used to prevent a terrible illness, somatic cell nuclear transfer is not done for any purported benefit to the child. Cloning would be done to satisfy the vanity of the nucleus donor or to serve the needs of someone else, such as a dying child in need of a bone marrow donor. In such cases, the child becomes an object, the means for the satisfaction of the wants of the person or couple who uses cloning. In addition, the rationale for using cloning, rather than other forms of reproduction, are to make the cloned child have very specific characteristics. The cloned child is supposed to be like a beloved child that died, or to be a genetic match for an organ transplant, or to express the mathematical or musical qualities of an exceptional person. Because the environment affects the ultimate make-up of a child, a cloned child may not necessarily achieve these standards.

Nevertheless, the reason the person or couple opted for somatic cell nuclear transfer was to create a child with specific characteristics, and the value of the child to them will depend upon meeting or expressing the desired characteristics and qualities. This is why some people worry that cloning would turn procreation and begetting into the making and manufacturing of children, that the humanity and dignity of children would be less respected, that children would be valued instrumentally rather than intrinsically.

Finally, opponents are concerned that permitting somatic cell nuclear transfer would affect not only how cloned children are treated and valued but the social understanding and norms surrounding family and parenting. Essential to good parenting and healthy families that contribute to the development of flourishing children are certain values – unconditional love, acceptance, openness, security, respect, recognition of individuality, etc.

The integrity of the family would be weakened because cloning would separate the genetic, gestational, and rearing parents of a child. The rearing father could be the genetic brother, with the rearing grandparents of a child being the genetic parents. Expectations about the obligations that the parties should assume, and society should morally expect and legally impose, would be uncertain. And, as we have seen with stored embryos, if conflicts develop – the parent rejects the cloned child or a divorce occurs – these uncertainties could become serious problems. Not only could this create legal difficulties, but also confused relationships, and uncertain duties could undermine a child's sense of security and belonging.

CONCLUSIONS

There are other arguments for and against cloning of human beings. Proponents point out that most of the objections are speculative and unproven and should not prevent a technique protected as a fundamental right and beneficial to individuals. Those opposed to cloning of human beings raise concerns about the use of cloning for eugenics, the transgression of moral boundaries as humans try to become God-like, and the inappropriate use of scarce resources.

RECOGNIZING AUTHOR'S POINT OF VIEW

This activity may be used as an individualized study guide for students in libraries and resource centers or as a discussion catalyst in small group and classroom discussions.

Many readers are unaware that written material usually expresses an opinion or bias. The capacity to recognize an author's point of view is an essential reading skill. The skill to read with insight and understanding involves the ability to detect different kinds of opinions or bias. **Sex bias, race bias, ethnocentric bias, political bias** and **religious bias** are five basic kinds of opinions expressed in editorials and all literature that attempts to persuade. They are briefly defined in the glossary below.

Five Kinds of Editorial Opinion or Bias

Sex Bias — The expression of dislike for and/or feeling of superiority over the opposite sex or a particular sexual minority.

Race Bias — The expression of dislike for and/or feeling of superiority over a racial group.

Ethnocentric Bias — The expression of a belief that one's own group, race, religion, culture, or nation is superior. Ethnocentric persons judge others by their own standards and values.

Political Bias — The expression of political opinions and attitudes about domestic or foreign affairs.

Religious Bias — The expression of a religious belief or attitude.

Summarize the author's point of view in one sentence for each of the following readings:

Reading 5_____

Reading 6_____

Reading 7_____

Reading 8_____

Reading 9_____

Reading 10 _____

Reading 11 _____

Guidelines

1. Locate three examples of *political opinion* or *bias* in the readings from Chapter Two.

2. Locate five sentences that provide examples of any kind of *editorial opinion* or *bias* from the readings in Chapter Two.

3. Write down each of the above sentences and determine what kind of bias each sentence represents. Is it *sex bias, race bias, ethnocentric bias, political bias* or *religious bias?*

4. Make up one-sentence statements that would be an example of each of the following: *sex bias, race bias, ethnocentric bias, political bias* and *religious bias.*

5. See if you can locate five sentences that are factual statements from the readings in Chapter Two.

CHAPTER 3

ANIMAL CLONING

READING

12

SOCIETY SHOULD BAN ANIMAL CLONING

Jeremy Rifkin

Jeremy Rifkin is president of The Foundation on Economic Trends in Washington, D.C., and author of Beyond Beef: The Rise and Fall of the Cattle Culture *(NAL/Durton).*

■ **POINTS TO CONSIDER**

1. Describe warnings given to scientists twenty years ago by the author.

2. Identify some troubling aspects of the biotech revolution.

3. What is meant by the phrase "shift from conception to replication?"

4. Why is Dolly's birth similar to the inventing of the printing press?

5. Why does Rifkin oppose animal cloning? How do you stand on this issue?

Jeremy Rifkin, "Dolly's Legacy: The Implications," **The Animals' Agenda**, May/June 1997: 34-35.

On February 23, 1997, the world was introduced to a seven-month-old Finn-Dorset Lamb named Dolly, the first known clone of an adult animal. A team of researchers led by embryologist Ian Wilmut at the Roslin Institute in Edinburgh, Scotland, kept Dolly's birth a secret long enough to publish a paper and secure a patent on their breakthrough technique. Unlike other animals who were cloned from embryonic cells, Dolly was "conceived" from the mammary cell of a six-year-old ewe, disproving the longstanding notion that a mature cell was not capable of growing and dividing.

Dolly's arrival has sparked much speculation and debate about cloning's potential benefits, as well as dangers, to humans. What has been lacking, however, is discussion of how this affects the well-being of animals – as individuals and as species. The Animals' Agenda asked author and activist Jeremy Rifkin for his thoughts:

Animal cloning is the most fundamental violation of animal rights in history.

Twenty years ago, at a gathering of molecular biologists sponsored by the National Academy of Sciences in Washington, D.C., I led a band of several hundred mostly young activists in what became the first protest of the fledgling science of biotechnology. We urged the scientists to consider the grave ethical, social, economic, and environmental issues raised by the new science, and warned that transgenic and chimeric animals, patented genes, surrogate parenting, and animal and human clones would likely be realized by the end of the 20th century.

At the time, scientists and much of the mainstream media ridiculed the protesters, accusing us of alarmism and sensationalism. Virtually every scientist attending the event said that such uses of biotechnology were unthinkable and, more importantly, undoable — at least in the next several hundred years.

Today, most of those youthful protesters are middle-aged or older, and memory of the event has faded. However, the issues have come back to haunt us as scientists have accomplished every one of the technological and commercial feats we warned of, except human cloning.

The recent revelation of the cloning of a mammal – the now famous sheep named Dolly – has briefly focused worldwide attention on some of the more troubling aspects of the biotech revolution. Still, in the frenzied public discussion following the announcement of Dolly's birth, very few commentaries have touched on the underlying significance of the story: the impact on the animals themselves.

REPLICATION

The shift from conception to replication marks the beginning of a new era in history. Until now, biological reproduction shared many similarities with art. Each organism born onto the Earth has been a unique creation, a living work of art. Now conception is merely an option. The cloning of mammals introduces replication into the biological process, and with it the specter of using engineering principles to both customize and mass produce identical copies of living organisms.

In this regard, Dolly's birth is as seminal an event in the emerging Biotechnical Age as was the invention of the printing press in the early Industrial Age. Before the printed book, written records were in the form of manuscripts, each painstakingly crafted by hand and bearing the unique characteristics and eccentricities of the scribes who dedicated their lives to keeping records. The printing press introduced the idea of mass replication of an original work, in a form that made the copies indistinguishable from the original.

BLUEPRINTS OF LIFE

The cloning of Dolly now forces humanity to consider the question of applying the same principles of industrial replication to the blueprints of life. Over the next decade, scientists expect to map the entire genome of many wild and domestic animal species, unlocking the inner mechanisms of their anatomy. The mapping of animal genomes will be followed, in short order, by the ability to engineer specific genetic traits into the egg, sperm, embryo, and fetus.

Together, cloning and genetic manipulation will allow scientists to both customize and mass produce animal offspring using the kind of quantifiable standards of measurement, predictability, and efficiency that have heretofore been used to transform inanimate matter and energy into a cornucopia of material goods.

Vegetarianism

Being a vegetarian contributes to your personal health as well as to the health of the planet. **Over 1/3 of the world's grain harvest is fed to animals raised for food.** By eliminating animal products, more grain would be available to feed the billion people suffering from chronic hunger.

Factory Farming

Over six billion animals are killed each year in the U.S. for food. Most of these animals are raised in confinement systems that severely restrict normal physical movement and social interaction. Most of the animals Americans eat never see daylight or breathe fresh air. Today's food production systems are deeply entrenched in animal exploitation.

Biomedical Research

Each year millions of animals are deliberately poisoned, shot, cut open, addicted to drugs, and killed in U.S. research laboratories. Billions of taxpayer dollars are wasted on animal models that have no direct relevance to human health. Significant physiological, anatomical, and biochemical differences between animals and humans contribute to the ineffectiveness of this kind of research.

Source: Animal Rights Coalition, Inc.

ANIMAL FACTORIES

Scientists and agribusiness companies hope to mass produce customized cloned animals both for use as chemical factories to secrete a range of drugs and chemicals, and for organ harvesting in medical research and human implementations. The meat industry is also interested in cloning; being able to reproduce animals with exacting standards of meat-to-fat ratios and other features, provides a form of quality control that has eluded the industry in the past.

What needs to be emphasized is that the idea of engineering animal species is not unlike the idea of engineering a piece of machinery. An engineer continually searches for new ways to improve the efficiency and performance of a machine. As soon as one set of imperfections is eliminated, the engineer turns his or her attention to new ways of improving performance, always with the idea of creating a more efficient machine. The very idea of setting arbitrary limits on how much "improvement" is acceptable is alien to the entire engineering concept.

PUBLIC DEBATE

The question that cries out for public debate is whether or not humanity should begin the process of replicating, customizing, and engineering future generations of our fellow creatures.

Animal cloning is a fundamental departure from both natural evolution and classical breeding, and ought to be prohibited on both ethical and environmental grounds. As stewards of our fellow creatures, we have a responsibility to protect the intrinsic value of all other forms of life as well as preserve the evolutionary wisdom of the age. Animal cloning risks undermining the biological diversity within each species that is essential to maintaining species viability into the future. The short-term commercial benefits of cloning both wild and domestic animal species could undermine the long-term survivability of our fellow creatures.

FINAL ANALYSIS

In the final analysis, animal cloning raises the formidable issue of the rights of our fellow creatures. Animal cloning is the most fundamental violation of animal rights in history. Reducing the animal kingdom to customized, mass-produced replications of specific genotypes is the final articulation of the mechanistic, industrial frame of mind. A world where all life is transformed into engineering standards and made to conform to market values is a nightmare, and needs to be opposed by every caring and compassionate human being who believes in the intrinsic value of life.

We need to pass immediate legislation in every country to outlaw animal cloning. Every creature has the right to be born into this world as a unique being able to experience the fullness of his or her essential nature, free of technological constraints and market-driven values. We have reached a point with the new biotechnologies where we need to say that just because it can be done, doesn't mean it should be done.

READING

13

ANIMAL CLONING SHOULD CONTINUE

Lester M. Crawford

Lester M. Crawford, D.V.M., Ph.D., was named director of the Georgetown University Center for Food and Nutrition Policy on July 1, 1997. Dr. Crawford had served as executive director of the Association of American Veterinary Medical Colleges (1993-1997) and, earlier, as executive vice-president of the National Food Processors Association (1991-1993). From 1987-1991 he was administrator of the Food and Safety and Inspection Service, U.S. Department of Agriculture. Dr. Crawford holds the Doctor of Veterinary medicine degree (Auburn University, 1963), the Ph.D. in Pharmacology (Georgia, 1969) and an honorary doctorate (Budapest, 1987). He is the author of over 100 scientific papers and has co-authored three books. He made the following statement on behalf of the National Association for Biomedical Research (NABR).

■ POINTS TO CONSIDER

1. Summarize the conclusions and finding of the National Bioethics Advisory Commission.

2. What limits should be placed on human cloning?

3. Discuss the kind of human cloning that should not be restricted.

4. Why should animal cloning continue?

5. Identify the great progress that will be possible with cloning and the new genetic techniques.

Excerpted from testimony by Lester M. Crawford before the Subcommittee on Technology of the House Committee on Science, July 22, 1997.

Research on cloning animals should continue. This type of research is both acceptable and beneficial to the public. Cloning techniques may benefit animals directly, either through improved medical treatments or by preserving genetic strengths.

I am here today as the Chairman-elect of the National Association for Biomedical Research Board of Directors. NABR, as the Association is called, is dedicated exclusively to advocating sound public policy regarding the humane and necessary use of animals in biomedical research, education and testing. NABR represents over 360 distinguished member institutions including the nation's largest universities, the majority of U.S. medical and veterinary schools, academic and professional societies, voluntary health organizations as well as pharmaceutical and biotechnology companies. We appreciate the opportunity to discuss the interests of the animal research community as they pertain to Congress' consideration of legislation concerning human cloning.

HUMAN CLONING

Like the other scientific organizations from which you have heard, NABR agrees with and supports the conclusions and recommendations made by the National Bioethics Advisory Commission (NBAC) in its June, 1997, report. Let me describe their findings as we understand them. The need to do this underscores the challenge facing this subcommittee and that is to clearly articulate our national policy governing the creation of a human being using somatic cell nuclear transfer. The three central actions that the Commission suggests be taken by government are:

First, attempts to create a human child using the new cloning technology of somatic cell nuclear transfer should not be permitted by anyone in the public or private sector, either in the laboratory or in a clinical setting. This prohibition is recommended not only because the technique currently is medically unsafe to use in humans, but also because there are moral and ethical concerns about this prospect that will likely continue to be deliberated and reviewed well into the future.

ANIMAL CLONING

Next, the use of somatic cell nuclear transfer in research on cloning animals should continue. This type of research is both acceptable and beneficial to the public. Existing animal welfare laws and regulations, including review by institution-based animal protection committees, are sufficient to address our concerns about animal research.

Likewise, additional limitations should not be placed upon the cloning of human cells and DNA sequences using somatic cell nuclear transfer. These research efforts do not raise the same scientific and ethical issues that surround the possible creation of an entire human being in the laboratory.

APPREHENSION & FEAR

It is understandable that an awesome achievement such as the birth of the lamb called Dolly, the first successful clone from an adult mammal somatic cell, has caused some degree of apprehension. What is not right is for the public's reasonable fears to be exploited by hyperbole. To this end, we in the research community must devote more attention to educating the public. With more reliable information, people will be prepared to separate legitimate science from science fiction. Unfortunately, in addition to some irresponsible, tabloid-type reporting on the subject of cloning, we have seen several radical groups try to recruit Dolly for their own propaganda purposes. One such group staged an anti-animal research demonstration during the NABC proceedings. The agenda of those few who would stop animal research in any way possible, for any reason whatsoever, must not cloud the important issues before you.

The Commission-supported continuation of the essential and responsible use of animals in biomedical research, and NABR is confident you will do the same in considering legislation regarding human cloning. More than this, NABR believes that the constructive hearing you and the Subcommittee are conducting will help alleviate needless apprehension and still encourage the best science. For the public expects research risks to be addressed while research benefits continue.

PROGRESS

Great progress in medicine and biotechnology is possible using new genetic techniques without entering the realm of cloning human beings. Genetically engineered mice have already revolu-

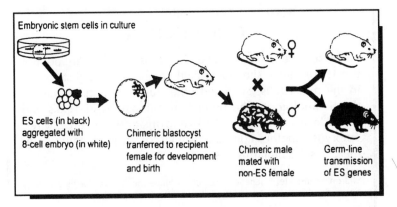

Embryonic stem cells in culture

ES cells (in black) aggregated with 8-cell embryo (in white)

Chimeric blastocyst tranferred to recipient female for development and birth

Chimeric male mated with non-ES female

Germ-line transmission of ES genes

Generation of mice from embryonic stem cells. Source: National Bioethics Advisory Commission.

tionized our ability to study devastating diseases such as breast cancer and immune system deficiency. Even better animal models for human disease, aiding research into new or improved therapies, are an exciting prospect stemming from the latest cloning methods.

The most immediate benefit is likely to be the faster, more efficient production of therapeutic human proteins in the milk of transgenic farm animal species. These drug products of biotechnology have already aided persons with blood deficiencies and serious infections among other conditions. In the longer-term future, cloned animals might become a safe source of organs for transplantation in patients with heart, kidney or liver failure.

Studying the somatic cell nuclear transfer process itself in animals and human tissue, never approaching the actual cloning of a human, could also provide other long-awaited answers. For example, so-called somatic mutations – mutations that take place in adult human and animal cells that are not inheritable – can cause tumors and other illnesses. Cellular changes of this type are also part of the aging process. Looking at the way cells undergo those sorts of mutations could help us better prevent cancer and avoid the negative effects of growing old, such as Alzheimer's disease. Ultimately, greater understanding of somatic cell differentiation might lead to the ability to regenerate or repair living tissue damaged by a variety of causes including spinal cord injury.

BENEFITS FOR ANIMALS

In veterinary and agricultural research, cloning techniques may benefit animals directly, either through improved medical treat-

> ## SCIENCE FICTION
>
> The science fiction of the early 1980s is at the barn door of the 1990s. Since sheep and cattle embryos were first cloned in the mid-1980s, Sims and other researchers have pushed the technology to the point that companies in Texas and Canada are selling elite breeding cattle from cloned embryos. Another company in Wisconsin is planning commercial sales on farms this decade.
>
> Sharon Schmickle, "Genetic Researchers Have the Answer for Finest Dairy Cows: Send in the Clones," **Star Tribune**, March 24, 1997, p. 1.

ments or by preserving genetic strengths. Rather than limiting genetic horizons, new technologies may help us to preserve biodiversity and ensure the continuation of rare individual animals or endangered species, too many of which are in need of protection today.

CONCLUSION

In summary, NABR believes that science and government have shared responsibilities. These duties are especially relevant to the national policy question now before you. Together we must reassure the public that:

- science will not pursue research results which society is morally and ethically unwilling to accept;

- research is being facilitated and the rewards of research can be enjoyed because safeguards are in place to protect humans and animals in experimentation; and

- existing laws and regulations are being followed and periodically reviewed to keep pace with new technologies.

NABR applauds you and the subcommittee for seeking a sound science policy regarding human cloning and trusts that in determining that policy you will promote responsible life-saving research. NABR would be pleased to provide any assistance you may need in the future to be certain that legislative proposals do not impede research requiring animals.

READING

14

THE SOCIAL COST OF ANIMAL CLONING

Michael W. Fox

Dr. Michael W. Fox joined the Humane Society of the United States (HSUS) in Washington, D.C., in 1976 and has produced numerous publications and developed several technical research programs that applied scientific methods to the investigation of the many uses of animals, notably laboratory, companion, and farm animals. He currently serves as Vice President of Bioethics for the Humane Society International and Senior Advisor to the President for the Humane Society of the United States. Dr. Fox has authored over 40 books and has a nationwide syndicated newspaper column, "Ask Your Animal Doctor." Dr. Fox has a veterinary degree from London's Royal Veterinary College, and a Ph.D. in medicine and a DSC in ethology/animal behavior, both from London University, England.

The Humane Society of the United States' primary and motivating concerns are the prevention of cruelty to all living creatures and the alleviation of all forms of animal suffering. Founded in 1954, The HSUS has a constituency and membership of near four million. You may reach The Humane Society of the United States at 2100 L Street NW, Washington, D.C. 20037. Phone: (202) 452-1100, Fax: (202) 778-6132.

■ POINTS TO CONSIDER

1. How are genetic defects a problem in animal cloning?

2. Identify how cloning might influence ways animals are used in the future.

3. Who was Dr. Ian Wilmut?

4. What process does the author wish to reverse?

5. Define the term *transgenic,* and tell how it relates to animal cloning?

6. What "brave new world" does the author see for animals and humans?

7. Define the term *anthropocentrism* and explain how the author uses it.

Excerpted from a paper by Michael W. Fox titled, "Cloning Animals in the New Animal Factories," September, 1997.

Animals are not on the agenda of human concern.

What is the point in cloning animals and where might it all lead? One immediate fear is that humans will be cloned once the technique is perfected. To date, only 29 of some 277 sheep embryos cloned by Dr. Ian Wilmut developed normally. Many died before birth, had defective kidneys, or were abnormally large – not the carbon-copy replicas the biotechnologist had anticipated. This animal welfare concern, as with creating transgenic animals through the invasive and crude techniques of genetic engineering, is neither effectively regulated nor addressed in most research reports.

UNIFORMITY

One real problem with creating animal clones is their genetic uniformity that is likely to decrease their survivability by increasing their vulnerability to infectious diseases. And another is the suffering of those animals afflicted by genetic and developmental defects caused accidentally, because the technology is not risk-free, or else they have been caused deliberately for biomedical research into human genetic and developmental diseases. Hundreds of varieties of genetically engineered *(transgenic)* mice have been created, many with such defects, and their suffering and welfare are precluded from consideration under the present federal Animal Welfare Act that excludes rodents from any protection.

EXPLOITATION

When cloning biotechnology is perfected, what will it mean for humans and other animals? The technique developed by Wilmut has been patented, so venture capitalists have high hopes that cloning will be a boost to the organ transplant industry and to pharmaceutical "pharming" of health care products. Pigs, and sheep, cattle, and goats have already been genetically engineered to serve respectively as organ donors for people and to produce more humanized milk, and milk containing valuable biopharmaceuticals. The numbers of these animals might now be rapidly increased using cloning biotechnology.

One ethical issue concerns the ever-intensifying commercial exploitation of animals as "biomachines" and as a source of replacement body fluids and parts for humans, from blood and bones to livers and hearts. These valuable patented human creations – "manimals" – of the new industrial biofarms of the next century will serve a wealthy elite. This may deter some extremely wealthy people from considering having themselves cloned for their clone to provide organ parts. "Manimals" instead will provide replacement body parts and vital elements as needed...

HUMAN CLONING

Senator Tom Harkin told the Senate Subcommittee hearings (convened by former heart-transplant surgeon Senator Bill Frist (R-Tenn.) that he vehemently opposed the President's cloning moratorium, proclaiming, "Human cloning will take place in my lifetime and I don't fear it. I welcome it, its untold benefits."

But Dr. Ian Wilmut, a slight, balding, bespectacled Englishman in his mid-40s, this brave new animal bioengineer from the small village Roslin Institute, close by the wild moors and glens of Scotland where a few natural sheep and shepherds try to hold on to a probably more sustainable way of life, challenged the Senator. He offered a rebuttal to Senator Harkin, stating he could see no reason to ever engage in the cloning of human beings and that an international moratorium should be put in place. Dr. Wilmut is a product of the late 20th century Industrial Revolution that is fusing commerce ever more destructively and intimately with the Earth's creation. This dominant culture is exploiting biodiversity, rushing for plant and other life patents, patenting transgenic animals and even patenting human cells and rare genetic types immune to certain diseases.

Now while I was in India on other Humane Society International (HSI) business when this story blew up, there were news reports of an Indian transplant surgeon who claimed to have successfully grafted the heart, lungs and kidneys of a genetically engineered pig into a patient (a sick human guinea pig from a shanty slum). However, the patient died of an infection a few days later, which this human vivisector of a doctor claimed was already sick with prior to the transplant being done. Because of the risk of transplant recipients becoming walking time bombs for new virus diseases that they might develop from contaminated animal organs, a moratorium on "xenografting" has been put in place in Europe. But there's nothing to stop a "mad" scientist from subjecting humans to biotechnological "enhancement" and self-replication through cloning.

TRANSGENICS

I see my task, as a bioethicist and veterinarian, to help reverse this process. We need to put our hearts into pigs and not pigs into ourselves. I would rather people become one with animals, through the heart's door of empathy, so that there may be more compassion in the world, rather than animals' parts and products becoming a part of our own bodies. This latter parasitic process and relationship only serves to demean and sicken the human spirit and condition. Where is there any respect or reverence for life when animals become bioengineered patented creations of the new animal "biofactories" of the 21st century? The dominant culture is using instrumental knowledge to manipulate and control life and increasingly direct the creative process to serve its own pecuniary ends. But without the balance of empathic knowledge – a deeper understanding and respect for the interrelatedness and interdependence of all life – the risks and costs of biotechnology are likely to far outweigh its benefits.

REVERENCE FOR LIFE

What of each animal's soul? What of the belief in reincarnation, held by over half the people of the world? What of the sanctity of life universal, not life in particular, in the simian-hominid Homo sapiens form? *Homo sapiens* means the wise being. I don't believe we are there yet. Without humility, empathy, and reverence for the sentience and sanctity of all beings, our sapience will surely be limited.

So I am very concerned that cloning biotechnology will be grossly misused for medically irrelevant and other ethically indefensible purposes, simply because they are lucrative ways to feed people, make them sick, and have them pay to get better. What of Peter the Pig Heart? (Long gone is Richard the Lion Heart!) Peter who took to the advertisements of the (publicly funded) National Pork Producers' Council to eat more of the "other white meat," and lots of crispy bacon and smoked Virginia ham too? Peter whose heart clogged up with the fat of denatured animal products, from pork sausage to cream cheese (from BGH-injected cows). Peter the pig heart recipient may require a xenotransplant psychotherapist and need a support group of kindred recipients of pigs' hearts coping with the psychological consequences of having an organ or more of another species in their bodies.

Companion Animals

Overpopulation has reached epidemic proportions: **over 20 million cats and dogs are euthanized each year in the U.S.** We actively promote spay/neutering and encourage support for local pounds and shelters. We discourage the purchase of animals at pet shops as many support the "puppy mill" industry.

Fur, Trapping, Hunting

Fur coats are no longer a status symbol, but rather **a symbol of cruelty.** Animals caught in traps often die a slow, agonizing death. Ranch raised animals fare little better. Bloodsports, such as hunting, encourage **disrespect both for animals and the environment.**

Source: Animal Rights Coalition, Inc.

BRAVE NEW WORLD

As a veterinarian, if I live another century or two, perhaps I might make house calls, along with a human bioengineer, to attend to some surrogate creature, providing vital antibodies, peptides, hormones and immuno-enhancers to owners, who keep the creatures as a kind of symbiotic pet. Or there may be thousands of such engineered and cloned sheep, pigs, goats, and cows pumping out proteins for drug and food manufacturing on the new biofarms, the "manimals" that veterinary college graduates of the next millennium will be trained to treat.

Cloning advocates may claim this biotechnology could help save endangered species by facilitating their replication in captivity. Can we preserve the natural by such unnatural means, and all to what end?

Cloning transgenic animals to manufacture new biopharmaceuticals preempts the development of humane production technologies and the application of existing ones, such as the use of genetically altered cells, bacteria and plants to achieve the same ends. Commercial-scale cloning will reinforce the demeaning perception of animals as disposable commodities of human creation. Patenting cloned, genetically engineered animals further erodes the ethic of respect for the intrinsic value and sanctity of individual life, an ethical principle that is critical to the future well-being of both humans and other animals.

ANIMAL WELL BEING

Aware of these and other potentially harmful consequences of cloning and genetic engineering biotechnology in general, the HSUS urged the President's National Bioethics Commission to consider animal well-being on its evaluation of all cloning applications, and to put a bioethicist informed about animal sentience, welfare, and behavior on the Commission.

We shall see. As I left the Senate hearings where I lamented in uncharacteristic silence the pervasive "anthropocentrism" and pro-biotechnology tenor of the entire proceedings, I met a science reporter and left feeling a little less alone. He told me he was deeply disturbed about the creation of genetically engineered animals, saying he was aghast at people "creating transgenic animals to maintain our depraved human existence."

TOOLS FOR TINKERING

"Artificially creating genetically identical monkeys for experiments further devalues the lives of these highly intelligent, sensitive animals and perpetuates the callous notion that they are nothing more than tools for scientific tinkering. Laboratory researchers who cruelly exploit non-human primates are out of step with an increasingly compassionate mainstream society."

Sheri Speede, Northwest Director, *In Defense of Animals,* September, 1997.

We have become depraved, I believe, by our own seduction into the kind of thinking Senator Bill Frist endorses, quoting the "father" of modern medicine, Dr. William Osler, in his Opening Statement: "To wrest from Nature the secrets which have perplexed philosophers in all ages, to track to their sources the causes of disease...These are our ambitions." Our anthropocentrism has disabled us from "tracking" at least half or more of the causes of disease that arise from us humans rather than from Nature. We still blame Nature for floods, famines and pestilence, yet most of these, like global warming and *E. coli* food poisoning from hamburgers, are anthropogenic.

FLAWED WORLD VIEW

Dr. Osler reflects the flawed world view of the dominant culture of bioindustrialism that has been obsessed with wresting from Nature the Dream of Francis Bacon (the 17th century founder of industrialism and prophet of biotechnology), namely, total control over life and the creative process. Perhaps Dr. Osler meant well, I'm sure, but his world view is as limited as the President's present Bioethics Advisory Commission. Animals are not on the agenda of human concern. Until they are, cloning and other developments in biotechnology are likely to do more harm than good and serve the interests of an increasingly depraved human existence.

It was evident from the Senate and Congressional hearings that the establishment is comfortable playing god with animals but not with ourselves. The bioethical questions about how far we can and should go in interfering with Nature, with life and Earth's creation, have yet to be openly and fairly addressed.

THE ADVANTAGES OF ANIMAL CLONING

National Bioethics Advisory Commission

The National Bioethics Advisory Commission was created in 1995 by the Clinton Administration to provide advice about research projects on human subjects sponsored by the federal government and to make recommendations about bioethical issues brought to its attention. The Commission issued a major report to the Nation on cloning, and the following reading was taken from this report.

■ POINTS TO CONSIDER

1. How will animal cloning be useful to humans?

2. What advantages does cloning bring for breeding livestock?

3. Define the term *transgenic* livestock, and explain how cloning might relate to these animals.

4. Why is the process of gene alteration important?

5. Identify the kind of animal research that will be useful to help do basic research on human disease.

Excerpted from "Cloning Human Beings," a report by the National Bioethics Advisory Commission, June, 1997: p. 24-29.

Basic research into these fundamental processes may also lead to the development of new therapies to treat human disease.

WHY PURSUE ANIMAL CLONING RESEARCH?

Research on nuclear transfer cloning in animals may provide information that will be useful in biotechnology, medicine, and basic science. Some of the immediate goals of this research are:

- to generate groups of genetically identical animals for research purposes

- to rapidly propagate desirable animal stocks

- to improve the efficiency of generating and propagating transgenic livestock

- to produce targeted genetic alterations in domestic animals

- to pursue basic knowledge about cell differentiation

ADVANTAGES OF NUCLEAR TRANSFER CLONING FOR BREEDING LIVESTOCK

In animal breeding, the rapid spread of certain traits within stocks of domestic animals is of obvious commercial importance and has very long historical standing. Artificial insemination and embryo transfer can increase the effective reproductive output of individual elite male and female animals and are widely used in the livestock industry. Nuclear transfer cloning, especially from somatic cell nuclei, could provide an additional means of expanding the number of chosen livestock. The ability to make identical copies of adult prize cows, sheep, and pigs is a feature unique to nuclear transfer technologies, and may well be used in livestock production, if the efficiencies of adult nuclear transfer can be improved. The net effect of multiplying chosen animals by cloning will be able to reduce the overall genetic diversity in a given livestock line, likely with severe adverse long-term consequences. If this technique became widespread, efforts would have to be made to ensure a pool of genetically diverse animals for future livestock maintenance.

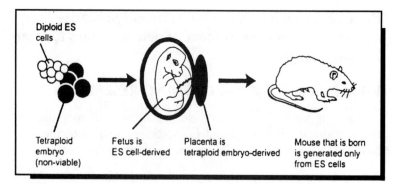

Diploid ES cells

Tetraploid embryo (non-viable)

Fetus is ES cell-derived

Placenta is tetraploid embryo-derived

Mouse that is born is generated only from ES cells

Mice can be generated directly from ES cells without first generating a chimera. Source: National Bioethics Advisory Commission.

IMPROVED GENERATION AND PROPAGATION OF TRANSGENIC LIVESTOCK

There is considerable interest in being able to genetically alter farm animals by introduction and expression of genes from other species, such as humans. So-called *transgenic animals* were first developed using mice, by microinjection of DNA into the nucleus of the egg. This ability to add genes to an organism has been a major research tool for understanding gene regulation and for using the mouse as a model in studies of certain human diseases. It has also been applied to other species including livestock. Proposed applications of this technology to livestock improvement include the possible introduction of growth-enhancing genes, genes that affect milk quality or wool fibers, or disease-resistance genes. But progress has been slow. Initial results of the manipulation of meat production by expression of excess growth hormone in pigs led to undesirable side effects.

Currently, the major activity in livestock transgenics is focused on pharmaceutical and medical applications. The milk of live-stock animals can be modified to contain large amounts of important proteins such as insulin or factor VIII for treatment of human disease by expressing human genes in the mammary gland. In sheep, greater than 50 percent of the proteins in milk can be the product of a human gene. Even the milk of transgenic mice can yield large (milligram) quantities of recombinant proteins. Since many such proteins are active at very low concentrations, it is estimated that production of human drugs from transgenic animals could be considerably more cost-effective than current methods.

CLONING RESEARCH

The continued pursuit of nuclear transfer as a means of producing genetically identical copies of embryonic or adult organisms has largely been driven by technological needs rather than by the pursuit of basic knowledge. The goals are:

1. To generate groups of genetically identical individuals for research purposes.

2. To rapidly propagate "elite" animal stocks.

3. To improve the efficiency of generation and propagation of transgenic livestock.

4. To generate targeted genetic alterations in domestic animals.

Janet Rossant, "The Science of Animal Cloning," A paper commissioned by the National Bioethics Advisory Commission, 1997.

Another major area of interest is the use of transgenic animals for organ transplantation into humans. Pig organs, in many cases, are similar enough to human organs to be potentially useful in transplants, if problems of rejection could be overcome. Rejection can already be partly overcome. Further transgenic manipulation, such as the expression of human antigens in pigs, could alleviate organ shortages by minimizing or eliminating the rejection of pig organs transplanted into humans, although other barriers, such as the possible transmission of viruses from pigs to humans, must be overcome.

The production of transgenic livestock is slow and expensive. Nuclear transfer would speed up the expansion of a successful transgenic line, but, perhaps more importantly, it would allow more efficient generation of transgenic animals in the first place. This, in fact, was the motivation behind the experiments that led to the production of Dolly.

BASIC RESEARCH

Basic research into these fundamental processes may also lead to the development of new therapies to treat human disease. It is not possible to predict from where the essential new discoveries will come. However, already the birth of Dolly has sparked ideas about potential benefits that might be realized. To explore the possibility of these new therapies, extensive basic research is needed.

Much of this basic research will likely be done in the mouse as this animal is widely used by developmental biologists, and thus a great deal is already known about its development. However, as described above, the use of cloning in other animals – such as cows, pigs and sheep – by agricultural and biotechnology companies will also contribute to understanding of the basic processes involved. The study of nuclear transplantation cloning in a wide variety of animals will be very useful. This body of research into animal systems will answer many questions about the feasibility of various new therapeutic applications being proposed for human cells. New innovations in treating human disease can be tested in animal systems to determine if the basic foundation of the idea is sound before experiments using human cells would be required. Thus the path to testing the potential therapies to treat human disease should initially go through testing in animal models before progressing to human cell research.

READING

16

ANIMALS NOT SUITABLE MODELS FOR RESEARCH ON HUMAN DISEASE

Physicians' Committee for Responsible Medicine

Physicians' Committee for Responsible Medicine wrote the following statement about the possible negative relationship between cloning and animal welfare. The Committee is located at 5100 Wisconsin Avenue, NW, Suite 404, Washington, DC 20016, Phone (202) 686-2210, Fax (202) 686-2216.

■ POINTS TO CONSIDER

1. Describe the likely applications that will result from the cloning of an adult animal in Scotland.

2. Why are animals not reliable models for studying human disease and illness?

3. Describe an alternative for the use of animals as models.

4. Explain how clone-generated organs for human transplant may present grave dangers to people in the future.

5. What happened to millions of people who received polio vaccines derived from monkey cells?

Excerpted from a public paper by the Physicians' Committee for Responsible Medicine titled, "Cloning Animals: A Step in the Wrong Direction," September, 1997.

Animals are not reliable or suitable "models" for studying human disease and illness.

Experimenters in Scotland recently declared that they have cloned an adult animal. This supposed "breakthrough" is nothing of the kind. Its applications are likely to waste time, effort, and money that could and should be better spent on preventive medicine, health education, epidemiological studies, and other human-centered research – programs that are proven to directly benefit human health.

- A similar report of cloning success appeared nine years ago, in 1988, in *The New York Times,* reporting that Angus cattle had been cloned in Alberta, Canada, as well as at the University of Wisconsin. However, agribusiness has not been revolutionized since that supposed breakthrough.

- Animals are not reliable or suitable "models" for studying human disease and illness, so having one more way to produce them is like finding a great new method to produce a Chevrolet Corvair. No matter how "revolutionary" the production process, what you're left with is a useless, unsafe, and unreliable product.

- Money and time would be better spent working with human cells – not cloning humans, but using isolated cells and cell clusters – which can be reproduced and kept alive in the laboratory. These cells, of course, behave exactly like their counterparts in a person and can be screened for human viruses, thus nearly eliminating the possibility of unleashing a new viral strain on humankind.

- The Multicenter for Evaluation of In Vitro Cytotoxicity (MEIC) has demonstrated that tests of isolated human cells match actual human experience with impressive accuracy. The human cell tests are clearly superior to similar animal tests. In one standard toxicity test, for example, results from rats were 59 percent accurate, but human cell tests reached accuracy levels of 80 percent.

- Experimenters claim these cloned sheep may someday produce organs for human transplant and human medicines. There is a grave danger that such uses could expose humans to unknown and deadly viruses. When an animal's genome is cloned, any and all viruses that animal harbors are also cloned. As was

Entertainment

Animals used for entertainment are subject to abuses that are hidden from the public. **Performing animals face lives of humiliation, stress, pain, and confinement.** Circus animals spend 75% of their lives in small traveling cages, thousands of greyhounds are killed each year in the racing industry, rodeo animals suffer severe injuries, and animals in zoos endure lives of boredom. Animals used in television and films, as well as other performing animals, often suffer behind-the-scenes cruelty from harsh training methods.

Product Testing

Many cosmetic and household product companies still perform archaic and unnecessary product tests on animals, including the Draize Eye Irritancy test in which substances are put into eyes of rabbits and may result in ulcers or blindness, and the LD-50 test in which substances are fed to test animals until 50% of the animals die. **Insist on cruelty-free cosmetics and household products.** Contact ARC for a list of cruelty-free companies.

Source: Animal Rights Coalition, Inc.

HUGE PROFITS

A Canadian researcher speaking at a farmers' convention eagerly tells the group that "at the Animal Research Institute we are trying to breed animals without legs and chickens without feathers."

Huge profits are to be made from new cows, pigs, chickens and other farm animals whose genetic scripts will be written and "improved" to grow faster and leaner on less food and on new foods such as sawdust, cardboard and industrial and human waste.

Carol Grunewald, "Monsters of the Brave New World," **New Internationalist**, January, 1991.

demonstrated recently, even genetically-engineered pigs, bred to be "germ-free" (gnotobiotic), harbor potentially deadly viruses (PERV, or "pig endogenous retrovirus") that can infect humans. This discovery led U.K. health officials to halt proposed animal-to-human organ transplant experiments.

- Millions of people who received polio vaccines derived from monkey cells in the 1950s were exposed to SV40 – a simian virus which has been "directly implicated in triggering cancer." (*New Scientist,* 8/24/96, p. 16) Since 1961, the vaccine has been screened for SV40, but prior to then, it was simply an unknown virus that came along for the ride when monkey cells were used to manufacture the vaccine. An estimated 10 to 30 million people in the U.S. received live SV40 before its discovery. Other unknown viruses could inhabit current animal-derived vaccines. If these cloned sheep are used to produce human vaccines or medicines, this scenario may well be repeated.

- Instead of throwing more money into animal-based vaccine research, promising research with plant-derived vaccines should be pursued. A paper recently published in *Nature Biotechnology* explained that plant-derived vaccines can protect animals from viral disease. Deriving vaccines from plant and/or synthetic sources eliminates the risk of transferring an animal-borne pathogen into people.

MASS-PRODUCTION

The experiment that led to Dolly was one of several conducted in Scotland and around the world to make the production of genetically altered, or transgenic, animals cheaper
and faster. Wilmut's new technology greatly improves corporate prospects for mass-producing animals that yield leaner
meat or more meat, generate high quantities of human proteins that can be harvested for the pharmaceutical trade, or
even provide spare parts for humans needing organ transplants.

Joni Praded, "Cloning: The Missing Debate," **Animals**, May/June, 1997.

- The bottom line is that animal tests do not correlate well with
  human data and experience, animal organs routinely fail when
  put into humans, and animal-derived vaccines and medicines
  could infect humankind with a host of new and deadly viruses.
  Instead of experimenting with this flawed system, our health
  and research dollars should go to preventing disease, health
  education, and exciting research with human cells and
  advanced molecular models that apply directly to humans.

READING

17

THE SCIENTIFIC BENEFITS OF CLONING ANIMALS

James A. Geraghty

James A. Geraghty has been the President and Chief Executive Officer of Genzyme Transgenics Corporation since its incorporation in February 1993. Mr. Geraghty joined Genzyme Corporation in September 1992 as Vice President of Corporate Development. He also served as General Manager of Genzyme's transgenics business unit until its incorporation as Genzyme Transgenics Corporation. Mr. Geraghty was previously Vice President of the Prescription Services of Caremark International which was then a unit of Baxter International. Prior to that, he held a variety of general management and strategy consulting positions with Bain and Company and with companies in the Bain venture capital portfolio. He holds a JD degree from Yale Law School, an MS from the University of Pennsylvania, and a BA from Georgetown University.

■ POINTS TO CONSIDER

1. How is transgenic technology described?

2. What kind of products will it produce?

3. Identify the important benefits of transgenic technology.

4. Discuss the relationship between cloning and transgenic technology.

5. Why does the author favor cloning? How do you feel?

Excerpted from testimony by James A. Geraghty before the Subcommittee on Technology of the House Committee on Science, March 5, 1997.

Benefits that animal cloning may add have and merit wide public support.

I am here to discuss transgenic technology and the potential impact that recent advances in cloning technology may eventually have on development and production. Cloning technology, like many other important scientific discoveries, poses great potential benefits to society as well as raising important ethical concerns. Let me say at the outset that I am confident everyone in the biotechnology industry shares the unequivocal conviction that there is no place for the cloning of human beings in our society. In these brief remarks, I would like to provide information on important transgenic research programs currently underway, and benefits that animal cloning may add, which I believe it is equally clear have and merit wide public support.

I. THE REALITY OF TRANSGENIC PRODUCTION

A. *Transgenic Technology*

Transgenic technology involves the transfer of genetic material from one species to another, and can be used for a wide range of medical purposes. Cloning may offer some potential for improving the efficiency of various applications of this technology. Let me give you some examples:

- Animals are being bred today whose organs may be transplanted into human patients suffering from organ failure, presenting some risk of immune system rejection. Cloning technology could potentially be used to make it easier to breed animals with organs that the human immune system would better accept.

- Another example lies in the development of genetically engineered animal models for use in testing potential treatments for various serious diseases. Cloning technology could allow for these animal models to be bred more quickly, which could in turn allow for research into curing a wider range of human diseases.

- As a final example, cloning technology may be useful in breeding animals that produce human therapeutic products. This is the focus of my company's work, which I would like to describe briefly.

B. *Production of Therapeutic Products*

Transgenic technology is widely used today to produce therapeutic proteins in the milk of dairy animals. At Genzyme
Transgenics, we have expressed more than 25 different proteins of
many different kinds. We are currently developing products for
the treatment of cardiovascular diseases, several forms of cancer,
diabetes, hereditary diseases, and others. We are presently
engaged in phase II clinical trials with a transgenic form of human
protein that helps prevent harmful blood clotting in many serious
medical conditions.

We produce these proteins by linking the gene that codes for
them to the gene that codes for a naturally occurring milk protein.
This construct is then injected into a one-cell animal embryo,
such that the new material can incorporate into the genetic make-
up of the resulting offspring. This integration does not occur in
every embryo, but about 10% of the animals born following injec-
tion will reliably incorporate the new material.

Once a transgenic animal has been born, the transgene will be
stably inherited by its offspring. The transgene has no effect on the
animals of any kind, except that when female offspring lactate, the
therapeutic protein is expressed in their milk along with native
proteins. This protein can then be purified away for the production of a pharmaceutical product.

C. *Importance*

There are several important benefits to transgenic production.
For some very complex proteins, transgenic technology presents
the only technically feasible way in which they can be manufactured. In addition, milk offers a safer alternative for products currently derived from sources such as pooled human plasma, which
necessarily carry some risk of transmitting infectious human diseases.

Furthermore, transgenic technology offers significant economic
advantages. Our production facility, on a 168-acre farm, can produce products for far lower capital and unit costs than the $100
million facilities often necessary to produce the same proteins
using conventional technology. Genzyme Transgenics has published widely on our work, and maintains an open dialogue with
and broad support from the scientific community, local communities, and the public.

REPLACEMENT ORGANS

Scientists have grown replacement organs for sheep, rats and rabbits using the animals' own cells and lab molds to help the tissue take shape – a technique that could be used someday to make spare parts for people.

While scientists already can grow skin and cartilage, two Harvard researchers say they are the first to have grown animal tissue from a variety of organs, including the heart, kidneys and bladder.

"Scientists Generate Replacement Organs from Animal Tissue," **Associated Press**, July, 1997.

II. THE POTENTIAL BENEFITS OF CLONING TECHNOLOGY

The cloning of animals has little application to transgenic production in the near term. This is the case both because large scale cloning is not commercially viable at this time, and because transgenic production is highly successful and fully viable without it. Longer term, cloning technology could further enhance the effectiveness of transgenic production in several respects. These include:

1. Enabling the breeding of a large number of offspring from a female founder in a single generation. This could allow the acceleration of herd expansion, clinical trails, and product launch.

2. Ensuring that all offspring bred from a founder are both transgenic and female. This could reduce the number of births, and therefore the costs, required to generate a full-size production herd.

3. Further insuring the biochemical identity of material from different animals, by eliminating variability in background genetic factors. This factor could be of greater value in areas such as the breeding of animals for organ transplantation.

It should be emphasized that these advances would represent incremental enhancements to more established if less well-publicized technologies. It is also possible that advances using other approaches will achieve some of these same objectives earlier or more effectively in the coming years. Finally, I would like to reiterate that all of these advances are fully achievable without any activities involving human cloning.

III. CONCLUSION

In closing, I would like to suggest what I believe could be the most significant opportunity presented by the birth of Dolly. As an event which has clearly captured the public imagination, this event offers a powerful platform from which to inform people about biomedical advances, and our understanding as to how life works. With such a focus, this moment offers the ability to engage an even broader community in a constructive dialogue about the benefits and acceptable limits of the technologies involved.

I believe that I speak for the biotechnology industry in thanking you for engaging in a constructive dialogue on these matters. We are always appreciative of the opportunity to update the American people about the continuing progress underway in biotechnology. Our industry is very conscious of the need to maintain an open dialogue, and to engage only in research and medical activities that are ethically responsible and acceptable to our society.

As Congress examines this issue further, we ask that it focus principally on mechanisms for further education and public participation in these fields. I join with others here in reminding the Congress that a rush to judgment in complex areas can easily lead to bad policy, and in urging it not to rush to legislation that might restrict widely accepted technology with great potential therapeutic benefits.

READING

18

THE PROMISE OF DOLLY:
POINTS & COUNTERPOINTS

Caird E. Rexroad, Jr., v.
The Humane Society of the United States

Dr. Caird E. Rexroad, Jr., is the research leader of the U.S. Department of Agriculture, Agricultural Research Service in the Gene Evaluation and Mapping Laboratory at the Livestock and Poultry Sciences Institute in Beltsville, Maryland. He argues for the "Promise of Dolly." The counterpoint to Caird Rexroad is given by The Humane Society of the United States which was organized to prevent all forms of cruelty to animals.

■ POINTS TO CONSIDER

1. How does Caird Rexroad define the "promise of Dolly?"

2. Why does animal cloning relate to the "promise of Dolly?"

3. According to The Humane Society of the United States, define the initial intent behind cloning.

4. Summarize our moral responsibility toward animals.

5. Describe your position on animal cloning.

Excerpted from Caird E. Rexroad, Jr., "The Promise of Dolly," **Agricultural Research**, May, 1997: p. 2, and a public statement on animal cloning by *The Humane Society of the United States,* September, 1997.

Statement of CAIRD E. REXROAD: The Point

Dolly, a sheep unremarkable except for her origin, has caused us to stop and think. Dolly, as the world knows, is the sheep cloned at Scotland's Roslin Institute. Since the formal announcement of her existence, there has been an intense public debate over the ethics of cloning both animals and humans. What hasn't been heard is the thinking behind Dolly's creation.

The scientists at Roslin Institute have conducted research for many years to produce rare drugs in the milk of sheep and cattle. That research was sparked by a U.S. Department of Agriculture (USDA) study that showed new genes, including human genes, could be inserted into sheep, pigs, and rabbits.

Some dozen years after this USDA study, the research at Roslin has begun to pay off. The Roslin scientists introduced into sheep a modified human gene that promotes production of the human protein alpha-1 antitrypsin. The Roslin scientists found that this human gene functioned in sheep and caused alpha-1 antitrypsin to be produced in the sheep's milk. The Scottish biotechnology company PPL Therapeutics has purified the human protein from the sheep milk and is testing it as a drug for the treatment of emphysema.

After seeing the power of this technology for alleviating human pain and suffering, many researchers sought support to conduct similar research on genes that produce other rare human proteins. Scientific reports indicate that human proteins for several blood clotting factors and for one antibacterial protein have been produced in animals' milk.

USDA's investment in research to understand genes and how they work appears to have produced an early payoff in biomedicine. Dolly represents a new approach to inserting genetic information into animals. How does this new approach improve on the method reported by USDA? In the earlier method, genes were injected into eggs. But the success rate was low. Less than one out of a hundred eggs would ultimately produce an adult animal with the inserted gene. Meanwhile, the investment in surrogate mothers for the 99 eggs that didn't carry the new gene made the research expensive.

In contrast, Dolly was produced from cells grown in the laboratory. In theory, if a new gene had been added to those cells, then all of Dolly's cells would have carried the new gene. Experiments are under way to test this assumption. It is possible that with appropriate germplasm conservation programs, we can design farm management programs to maximize the consistent qualities of a set of clones.

Returning to the issue of the benefits of cloning – will we produce much of our lean meat from clones? It seems unlikely, at least for a while. Producing Dolly was expensive and inefficient. Also, we must protect the genetic diversity of our food-producing animals so they can respond effectively to challenges such as emerging diseases or climatic change. If all animals were genetically identical, they would all have the same vulnerabilities.

We in USDA's Agricultural Research Service expect to put the methods that produced Dolly to a variety of uses. For example, they might help us learn more about the genes behind whether an animal uses food to make muscle or fat and about the genes that control a cow's level of resistance to mammary gland infections. They will aid the study of methods to make milk an even healthier food for people – especially infants – and there will be other studies that we have yet to envision. Just as the basic research at USDA was the predecessor to Dolly, the new research made possible by Dolly will ultimately pay off in many ways, for animals and people alike.

Statement of THE HUMANE SOCIETY OF THE UNITED STATES: The Counterpoint

Following the revelation of the existence of Dolly, the first clone of an adult mammal, President Clinton has requested the National Bioethics Advisory Commission to immediately examine related biotechnology research and animal husbandry issues. The Humane Society of the United States, on behalf of its 4.1 million members and constituents, urges that animal suffering be rightfully considered in this evaluation.

The initial intent behind cloning is to produce large numbers of genetically identical animals who will become production "machines," pumping out proteins that are already being obtained more humanely from genetically altered yeast, bacteria, and mammalian cells. Cloning also aims to create more animal "models" for invasive biomedical research.

Cloning animals will accelerate the trend toward factory "farming," causing more animal confinement, crowding and suffering. Genetic diversity will also be reduced, rendering herds more susceptible to being wiped out by disease. Dr. Kevin FitzGerald, a Jesuit priest and a geneticist at Loyola College cautions, "An entire cloned herd could be wiped out overnight if the right virus swept through it."

Society needs to realize that cloned animals are no less sensitive to physical and psychological suffering, and that our moral responsibility toward them is no less than for other animals. The demeaning perception of animals as "nothing but cells on the hoof" and irrelevant in discussions of bioethical concerns inevitably leads to a lack of respect and compassion.

The secrecy behind this and other genetic engineering experimentation is particularly disturbing, the announcement having sent shock waves through scientific and bioethics communities worldwide. Previously known only to a select few, Dolly was actually born seven months ago, and eight other sheep have also been cloned. Prior genetic experimentation, which has also been presented as being benign to the animals involved, instead resulted in animals with arthritis, lethargy, defective vision due to abnormal skull growth, gastric ulcers, pneumonia, seriously impaired immune systems and high mortality.

The White House has called the cloning issue a "very troubling subject;" Nobel peace prize winner Joseph Rotblat has compared it with the creation of the atom bomb. Dr. Lee Silver, a biology professor from Princeton University has stated, "It's so typical for scientists to say they are not thinking about the implications of their work." Perhaps speculation that the market for therapeutic proteins will more than double, increasing by $10 billion within the next three years, more accurately reflects some of the impetus behind research that is not only unnecessary and disturbing to the public, but which also carries with it so many important and unaddressed ethical questions.

It is very possible that humans will suffer from genetic engineering. It is certain that animals already do. The public is entitled to a full review of this very problematic issue, and animal welfare needs to be part of that consideration.

INTERPRETING EDITORIAL CARTOONS

This activity may be used as an individualized study guide for students in libraries and resource centers or as a discussion catalyst in small group and classroom discussions.

Although cartoons are usually humorous, the main intent of most political cartoonists is not to entertain. Cartoons express serious social comment about important issues. Using graphic and visual arts, the cartoonist expresses opinions and attitudes. By employing an entertaining and often light-hearted visual format, cartoonists may have as much or more impact on national and world issues as editorial and syndicated columnists.

Points to Consider

1. Examine the cartoon on page 41.

2. How would you describe the message of the cartoon? Try to describe the message in one to three sentences.

3. Do you agree with the message expressed in the cartoon? Why or why not?

4. Are any of the readings in Chapter Three in basic agreement with the cartoon?

CHAPTER 4

RELIGIOUS TRADITIONS AND CLONING

A COMPARISON OF RELIGIOUS VIEWS ON CLONING

Courtney S. Campbell

Courtney S. Campbell, Ph.D., is a professor of philosophy at Oregon State University. His following statement comparing religious views on cloning was commissioned by the U.S. National Bioethics Advisory Commission.

■ POINTS TO CONSIDER

1. Why are people in Native American Religious Tradition suspicious of cloning?

2. Compare Buddhist views on cloning with those of Native Americans.

3. Summarize Hindu thought toward cloning.

4. In Islam, what is the meaning of the terms *sunni* and *Shi'ite?*

5. Compare and contrast Islamic and Jewish thinking on cloning.

6. Explain the diversity of thinking on cloning among the various Protestant faith traditions.

7. Which religious traditions are the most suspicious of cloning? The least suspicious?

Excerpted from Courtney S. Campbell, "Examinations of Views of Religious Traditions on Issues of the Cloning of Humans," May, 1997.

RELIGIOUS TRADITIONS

This section contains specific information on the views of distinctive religious traditions regarding ethical questions in human cloning research. With very few exceptions, the religious traditions discussed here have yet to develop specific theological or denominational positions on the moral or public policy aspects of human cloning.

In considering the implications of these religious positions for public policy on human cloning, it may be useful to adopt the metaphor of a traffic semaphore.

- *"Red"* indicates a full stop to research and/or cloning. The policy analogue is a permanent moratorium or prohibition.

- *"Flashing Red"* indicates the need to stop to evaluate risks before proceeding. The policy analogue is a temporary moratorium until important scientific and social questions are addressed.

- *"Amber"* indicates the need to proceed with caution and care, slowing the pace of, or stopping, research as necessary. The policy analogue is a regulatory model coupled with the adoption of guidelines by relevant professional bodies.

- *"Green"* indicates permission for cloning research and/or cloning on the assumption that other stakeholders in human cloning will conform to norms of professional and social responsibility. The policy analogue is the adoption of guidelines by relevant professional bodies.

Given the diversity of American religion, an inherent risk of the following analysis is oversimplification. The discussion nonetheless should indicate important questions raised by religious communities and thinkers about science, technology, and human cloning.

NATIVE AMERICAN

It is worth recalling that the source of philosophical critique in Huxley's **Brave New World** *was Native American culture. Native Americans do not partition religion from other life domains; rather, religion is a "way of life." Good health requires living in conformity with the ways of life Native Americans received at the time of creation. The whole of creation is good within Native American narratives, and all creation is animated, interrelated*

*and responsible for harmonious interaction to sustain the order
of life in the world.*

*Within this world view, Native Americans give primacy to the
good of the whole, or the group, rather than to alleged needs of
individuals. Individual actions must be placed within a holistic
perspective; as with a pebble that causes a ripple effect in an
entire body of water, so there are no isolated actions that do not
have repercussions on the greater whole.*

Life Balance. Illness is a result of disorder or imbalance between
persons, or between persons and nature, or within a person. The
aim of traditional healing practices is to restore balance and order
to the person. Ritual, ceremony, and language are no less important to maintaining or restoring health. A study of the Navajo
found that thought and language were potent forces for the shap-
ing of reality, for better or ill.

Cloning Research. Animal cloning, and the potential for human
cloning, risks substantial disruption of the created order and balance. Animal research erodes the reverence and kinship between
humans and other created beings. Cloning research on human
embryos symbolizes the Western, non-Native pursuit of technical
solutions. Moreover, these technological skills are not accompa-
nied by necessary practical wisdom about the ways of life. Sakim,
a traditional elder from the Muskogee tribe observes of cloning:
"We are becoming more like Creator with every day that goes by.
However, it is only our abilities that are growing that way. We are
not blessed with nor in any manner fraught with the judgment of
Creator. That is the fundamental problem."

Resource Priorities. Fertility drugs, other methods of reproductive
technology, and cloning can disrupt the balance of communal co-
existence. This communal balance relies on an acceptance that
human beings and groups exist in a bounded space that may not be
expanded. The human species as a whole has nonetheless expanded beyond its given bounds through overpopulation; cloning simply
will perpetuate a problem of human growth and increasing scarcity
of those resources needed to live a decent human existence. In this
context, "the application of the knowledge to clone a human being
is unjustified" (Cordova). In particular, a focus on scientific technology such as cloning will divert needed attention and resources
away from basic care for Native Americans, whose life expectancy
is the shortest of any demographic group. The needs of a few cannot be prior to the good of the whole.

Indigenous Cultures. What support that does exist among Native American culture for human cloning may pertain to the preservation of endangered indigenous peoples. The Rev. Abraham A. Akaka, a Native American Hawaiian pastor, has commented: "For aboriginal people of our planet who see themselves as a dwindling and endangered species, cloning of the best of their race will be a blessing – a viable avenue for preserving and perpetuating their unique identities and individualities upon lands they revere as Father and Mother" (Akaka). This qualified support for human cloning is consistent with the Native emphasis of maintaining the balance of the ways of life given to peoples at creation. It does not, however, warrant individualist desires for cloning that have little bearing on the perpetuation of a species or culture.

Cloning Research: *Flashing Red*

Human Cloning: *Flashing Red*

BUDDHISM

The Buddhist Churches in America claim approximately 100,000 adherents. There are, in addition, numerous non-affiliated Buddhist temples, monasteries, and organizations. There is as yet no systematic consideration of cloning by Buddhist scholars, nor is there any formal teaching authority. This manifests the Buddha's warning to his followers that speculation about metaphysical issues was futile because the human problems of birth, old age, death, and sorrow remain regardless. However, basic Buddhist teachings present an ethic of responsibility, centered on the values of non-injury and the relief of suffering, compassion, the moral authority of intuition, and reincarnation. These values offer some elements of a Buddhist response to reproductive and genetic technologies, including cloning.

Buddhist teachings indicate that the Buddha (560-477 BCE) provided a four-fold decision-making method for his followers should they encounter unanticipated questions. The four steps involve recourse to (1) original Buddhist texts; (2) derivation of rules in harmony with the original texts; (3) the views of respected teachers; (4) the exercise of personal judgment, discretion, and opinion. Buddhist scholars have cited this method as a resource for Buddhists in addressing the issues of cloning, with a particular emphasis on the authoritative nature of personal intuition and opinion (Nakasone). By its nature, then, there is a notable diversity of views by Buddhists on cloning, rather than a Buddhist view.

Procreation and Reproduction. Buddhist scholars generally agree that the process by which children are born into the world makes no difference. "Individuals can begin their lives in many ways," including but not limited to human sexual generation. Cloning is thereby understood as an alternative method of generating new human life, in principle continuous with other methods (Keown). One Buddhist ethicist has supported use of reproductive technology, so long as it benefits the couple who wish to have a child, and does not bring pain or suffering. However, some Buddhist scholars find in human cloning an impoverished approach to procreation. It marks a diminished creativity and diversity, analogous to the difference between the creativity, initiative, and investment that is required for an original painting, and the mechanistic process required to reproduce the painting.

Human Status and Enlightenment. The status of the human being is critical within Buddhist thought because it is the only condition by which an entity can achieve "enlightenment" and liberation from a world marked by suffering. Buddhist scholars throughout history have reiterated that, due to *karma,* the chances of being born as a human being are rare and remote. Human life is a precious opportunity to escape from perpetual rebirth *(karma-samsara)* by following the teachings *(dharma)* of the Buddha.

In this respect, any form of human reproduction, sexual or asexual, that allows for the birth of a human being may be especially valuable. Buddhist tradition contains stories of "spontaneous generation." Buddhist scholar Damien Keown states that cloning, if it "is ever perfected in human beings, would show only that there are a variety of ways in which life can be generated.

Some forms of Buddhism may endorse cloning because of the chance human life gives to achieve enlightenment. The Dalai Lama, the exiled leader of Tibetan Buddhism, was questioned about his attitude towards the following hypothetical scenario: "What if at some future time...you could make by genetic engineering, with proteins and amino acids, or by engineering with chips and copper wires, an organism that had all of our good qualities and none of our bad ones...?" The Dalai Lama indicated he would welcome such a technological development because it would facilitate the process of rebirth and liberation.

Moral Development and Spiritual Priorities. Buddhist understandings that change is the nature of reality suggest that, in considering technological developments, the central questions concern how persons can accommodate change, and how they can use change to expand their self-understanding and their understanding of humanity. Cloning may be an occasion for self-knowledge, which is a central feature to the experience of enlightenment. Nonetheless, the end of enlightenment may not, for some Buddhists, justify the use of any means of reproduction.

Moreover, while cloning may preserve genetic identity, it cannot assist in, what for Buddhists is most critical, the cultivation of spiritual identity. This misguided priority is reflected in the statement of Gen Kelsang Tubpa, a Buddhist monk: "Cloning is just another example of man's belief that by manipulating the external environment, he will create happiness for himself and freedom from suffering."

Some Buddhist scholars have raised objections to applications of cloning, particularly commercial or social agendas that may support cloning for reasons contrary to the interest of the clone. These agendas may include pressures on scientists for continual progress and discovery or commercial gain from pharmaceuticals or organ harvesting. In this respect, there would be greater suspicion within Buddhism about private-sponsored cloning research without public oversight.

Sentience and Cloning Research. While cloning might be permissible under some understandings of Buddhism, the scientific research necessary to build up to cloning encounters difficulties. Part of the "Noble Eightfold Path" promulgated by the Buddha prohibits infliction of violence or harm on sentient (perceptive) beings. Moreover, especially where the research process is very inefficient and causes loss of life, both embryo research and animal research would be especially problematic. Any Buddhist account would ask of cloning research or human cloning: "How does this serve all sentient beings?"

Cloning Research: *Flashing Red*

Human Cloning: *Amber*

HINDUISM

"Hinduism" is a western term for a family of philosophies and religious practices that have their origins in the Aryan period of Indian history and the Vedic scriptures (1200 BCE). There is no formal teaching authority for the world's one billion Hindus

124

(Hindu population in the United States is estimated at two million). However, classical texts and commentary have offered four principal values: Dharma (virtue, morality); Artha (wealth, power), Kama (aesthetics, sexuality), Moksa (liberation) to guide Hindu life. Liberation from the cycles of rebirth is the ultimate goal within Hinduism, while Dharma regulates the pursuit of Artha and Kama. Using these values, scholars of Hinduism and Hindu practitioners have begun to initiate ethical discourse on a wide array of social practices in India and North America, including those of cloning.

Self. Classical Hinduism does not accept distinctions found in Western thought between God, human beings and other creatures, or between the supernatural, human nature, and nature. Rather, the self (*atman*) is part of the creative force (*Brahman*) and life energy residing in all creation. Hinduism affirms a oneness of self with divinity rather than separation. A person cannot "play God" because in an ultimate sense the self is God. Hindu texts describe the *atman* as pure spirit. It is "eternal, free from disease, free from old age, deathless, free from decay; it cannot be pierced, cut or agitated" (Lipner).

Two concepts of relevance for issues of cloning may be inferred from this religious anthropology. First, if the real self or true consciousness is radically distinct from the body, it is beyond the reach of material science and hence cannot be harmed by genetic manipulations or cloning. A second principle is that scientific processes and methods (though not their practical application) manifest the workings of divine consciousness.

Creation by Cloning. Values embedded in Hindu narrative tradition may offer the community analogues to human cloning. Hindu creation narratives are replete with references to the creation of a person, a deity, or social groups through cells of skin or drops of blood. However, in a classic narrative, the *Ramayana*, only demonic persons *(asuras)* come from divine blood. This suggests to some Hindu spiritual leaders that society has little control over ensuring only good outcomes of cloning.

Cloning Research. The animating spirit is present from fertilization in classical Hindu thought. Biological development does not shape moral development, however, for the embryo is given the status of person throughout pregnancy. Hindu thought is thus concerned with moral attitudes towards research on the pre-embryo; in particular, such concerns would focus on exploitation of the vulnerable, and whether the underlying dispositions could be limited to the research setting, or would influence how human beings treat each other and treat animals.

The *Dharma* gives great authority to *ahimsa*, or the non-injury of sentient beings. This inclusive scope of beings within the moral community renders much contemporary animal research without justification. Animal research for the benefits of animals can be justified, but it is more difficult to justify when such research is conducted solely to advance human interests.

Human Cloning. Some Hindu scholars may permit human cloning under very circumscribed or exceptional circumstances. The primacy of generational continuity, especially the establishment of father-son lineage, is underscored in the *Mahabharata* (an Indian epic analogous to the *Odyssey*). Other scholars maintain that the four values of Hinduism would support human cloning when it is conducive to material or spiritual well-being, such as to alleviate infertility or for saving life through providing compatible bone marrow *(Sharma)*.

Life Priorities. Within any Hindu discussion of cloning, there is concern that scientific attention on cloning will divert attention from the true purpose of life, which is to become conscious of and actualize one's self in union with the divine. Sri Easwaran has suggested the question we need to ask in the light of significant scientific discoveries such as the splitting of atoms or of cloning is: "Will this help me in my search for realizing God, who is enshrined in the depths of my consciousness?"

The cultivation of spiritual self-awareness, rather than manipulation of the external environment, or one's biological self, which is no less an external organic environment, is the overriding concern of the Hindu tradition. Human cloning thereby suggests the wrong questions are being asked about life's meaning and about social priorities.

Cloning Research: *Flashing Red*

Human Cloning: *Flashing Red*

ISLAM

Islam ("submission") is the youngest of the Abrahamic family of religions (Judaism, Christianity, Islam). Islam presents continuity with Judaism and Christianity – Abraham and Jesus are

126

"prophets" in Islamic tradition – as well as distinctiveness, which stems from the reevaluation of the Qur'an to the Prophet Muhammad *(610 CE)*. The two main sub-traditions of Islam are Sunni *(about 80%)* and Shi'ite *(about 20%)*. Within the United States, the Muslim population is estimated to comprise between three to six million persons. Islam does not recognize a separation of religion, ethics, law, and politics; rather, Islamic law or Shari'a regulates belief, worship, the family, and personal and social morality.

Science and Technology. The pursuit of knowledge, including scientific inquiry, receives a divine warrant in Islamic thought. Indeed, the Islamic Code of Medical Ethics portrays the pursuit of knowledge as worship of God. Scientific discoveries do not threaten God as much as they reveal the intricacies of God's creation and will to humanity. Scientific research and investigation in most circumstances should not be curbed, and human interventions in nature are permissible to promote health.

However, Islam does not view technology as morally neutral. Instead, Islam believes careful consideration must be given to potential abuse. Islamic traditions thereby express significant moral concern regarding the potential for discrimination in a sinful world, especially stemming from political and economic systems that do not give primacy to the promotion of human dignity. Islamic discussions of human cloning have also emphasized the possibilities for evil present in the pursuit of knowledge and of persons through motivations of profit.

Therapeutic Research. The *Qur'an* describes persons who reject God and follow Satan as persons who "will change God's creation" (4:119). This has caused leading Sunni authorities in Saudi Arabia and Egypt to condemn cloning as "the work of the devil" and advocate punishment for scientific researchers. However, Islamic jurists in general have not interpreted this *Qur'anic* passage to preclude forms of genetic intervention, such as somatic cell therapy, provided that such interventions are done for therapeutic purposes and are life-promoting in intent. The question Islam poses to proposals for human cloning is in what sense such research can legitimately be described as therapeutic (dealing with treatment and cure).

Schools of Islamic thought have not provided a consensus on the moral status of the human embryo. Some traditions affirm that ensoulment occurs at fertilization, whereas other traditions indicate ensoulment occurs at the end of the fourth month (120 days) following fertilization. Within these latter traditions, it becomes possible to argue for research on the human pre-embryo for purposes of human health. Moreover, if the embryo is not accorded personhood, then destruction of the embryo is permissible.

Relationships. While Islam warrants biomedical research and clinical application for therapeutic purposes, issues of the integrity of relationships have raised questions about the legitimacy of reproductive technologies. The tradition gives special attention to preserving spousal, procreative, and parenting relationships because of designated role-responsibilities within the *Shari'a*. Use of third-party gametes for reproduction violates precepts concerning legitimacy, lineage, and inheritance. Transformed relationships can confuse relationships and their correlative responsibilities. These values, and objections to third-party assisted reproduction, would extend to cloning of human beings. Nonetheless, use of cloning research as an aid to fertility within the bounds of marriage would likely be substantially supported by Islamic scholars and traditions (Sachedina).

The *Shari'a* (Islamic Law) also places moral priority on refraining from harm over the production of benefits. The formation of public policy on a medical technology then must place the burden of proof on those who advocate technological innovation to establish clear benefits and to weigh immediate and prospective long-term harms.

Cloning Research: *Amber*

Human Cloning: *Flashing Red*

JUDAISM

Judaism is the oldest of the Western monotheistic faith traditions. Its primary source of authority is the Torah, *the revealed will of God in the* Hebrew Bible, *and rabbinic commentaries on the Torah contained in the* Talmud *and* Mishnah. *Within the United States, there are four main Jewish traditions – Conservative, Orthodox, Reform, and Reconstructionist – that collectively claim approximately three% of the U.S. religious population. Jewish scholars have drawn on their authoritative sources and reasoning to make substantial contributions to biomedical ethics since its inception. Indeed, discussion of human cloning by Jewish scholars begins to appear in the late 1970s.*

128

The Divine Mandate and the Self. Human beings have a command and challenge from God to use their rational, imaginative, and exploratory capacities for the benefit and health of humanity. Judaism affirms that human beings have inherent worth as creatures created in the image of God, and the Talmud understands human beings as partners with God in the ongoing act of creation. In their unique role, persons receive a divine mandate for stewardship and mastery, which encompasses a very strong emphasis on use of medical knowledge and skills to promote health, cure and heal.

Nonetheless, the divine mandate of mastery generates moral ambivalence in the tradition with respect to cloning. Cloning is troubling because of the prospect that the mandate to master nature will be transformed into mastery over man. The Jewish understanding of the self entails that the person is more than his genotype. Rabbi Jakobovits has highlighted the transcendent character of the person within Jewish thought: "…man, as the delicately balanced fusion of body, mind, and soul, can never be the mere product of laboratory conditions and scientific ingenuity." Jewish perspectives on cloning are also profoundly influenced by the eugenics programs carried out on European Jewry under Nazi Germany.

An Ethic of Responsibility. Judaism is committed to an ethic of responsibility or duty, rather than an ethic of rights. The overriding duty (with three exceptions), derived from the *Torah* and rabbinic commentary, is the preservation of human life. Given this presumptive duty, it is possible to support cloning when it is presented as a therapeutic remedy for a genetic disease or condition, such as infertility, that besets an individual or couple. However, many proposals for human cloning do not meet these conditions of underlying disease, therapy, and individual benefit.

One exception to the command to preserve life, the prohibition of idolatry, is relevant to an assessment of cloning. Human cloning raises a danger of self-idolization. Through sexual intercourse and the raising of children, human beings are confronted with the inescapable "otherness" of persons. This otherness enables the development of humility and the authenticity of "I-Thou" relationships. These characteristics curb human *hubris* and self-idolization (Dorff).

The ethic of responsibility is also expressed in Jewish norms of parenthood and the responsibilities of lineage. In the context of human cloning (or other reproductive technologies), the ethic of responsibility would be diminished because of changed roles (father, mother, child) and relationships (spousal, parental, filial). It would be unclear who has responsibilities to whom between and among the generations. According to Rabbi Tendler, "we do not live well with generational inversion" that might be induced by cloning.

Status of a Clone. One source invoked by some Jewish scholars to inform community reflection are the *Golem* narratives in Jewish mysticism. The Golem narratives describe the creation of artificial, human-like life by a mystic. The narratives are deemed to present parallels to human cloning insofar as they implicitly address the status of human life without direct human parentage. However, were a human clone to be actually produced from biomedical research, there is rabbinic consensus that the clone would have human status and the imperative to protect life would require protection and care for the clone.

Cloning Research. Jewish scholars are wary of a public policy prohibiting cloning research, which would violate the command of mastery, interfere with valuable scientific research, and compromise public oversight and accountability. It is considered important to pursue scientific research that precedes cloning because of its potential benefits. Since Jewish law does not grant full moral status to the human embryo, cloning research conducted on the early human embryo can be warranted; however, a high incidence of embryo deaths, attributable to the inefficiency of research, would violate the maxim of do no harm.

Human Cloning. The prospect of human cloning elicits ambivalence but seldom direct condemnation in Jewish scholarship; the ambivalence is expressed in a *Talmudic* maxim that, at some point, human beings must ask whether they are prepared to forgo the honey from a bee in order to avoid the sting (Tendler). Jewish scholars support extensive consideration by the Jewish community of the ethical and social issues pertaining to human cloning. Rabbinic discussion does express fundamental concerns about the potential commercializing of human life through cloning. Insofar as cloning, coupled with capitalistic motivations, transforms the person into a product or fungible commodity, it would violate the sacred character of human life.

Cloning Research: *Amber*

Human Cloning: *Amber*

PROTESTANT CHRISTIANITY: MAINLINE

The religious witness of mainline Protestantism focuses on questions of peace and social justice rather than the right-to-life. The seven principal denominations designated as "mainline" (American Baptist, Christian Church [Disciples of Christ], Episcopal, Evangelical Lutheran, United Methodist, Presbyterian, United Church of Christ) Protestant claim approximately 17% of the U.S. religious population.

These denominations have been very active in developing ecclesiastical position statements and convening working groups to address theological and ethical issues in biomedicine. Moreover, ecclesiastical leaders and theologians have been prominent in bringing such issues to the consideration of more global bodies, such as the National Council of Churches in Christ and the World Council of Churches. However, the primacy of freedom of conscience in Protestantism means that theologians engaged in biomedical ethics may not agree with the views of denominational bodies or their theological peers. This summary will reflect this theological diversity rather than resolve it.

Creative Freedom. An important question within mainline Protestant thought is whether there are any adequate precedents to guide ethical reflection for the advent of reproductive and genetic technologies, or what one scholar has described as the "new genesis." A first position affirms that we are free to engage in exploratory ethics because human destiny lies in the future rather than being determined by the past. Theological ethics begin by God giving human beings a future to shape and create in partnership with God. Genetic and reproductive technologies express the creative dimensions insofar as they promote human dignity and welfare. Within this understanding, no theological principle stands as a bar to human cloning.

Research Criteria. A second position distinguishes between the ethics of cloning research and the ethics of cloning human beings for purposes of transfer and birth. Research on cloned embryos can be justifiable, using the precedent of current standards for the regulation and protection of human and animal subjects. However, cloning of humans involves creation after our image rather than God's and can lead to power over humans rather than enhanced choices. Decision-makers should instead focus on the interests of children, that is, on those persons living in the future created for them. At a minimum, society should engage in a sustained and substantive debate on the possible benefits and the likely harms of human cloning, with a burden of proof imposed on the research community to establish a compelling case for the beneficial and therapeutic uses of the technology.

Research Moratorium. Public discourse is necessary but insufficient: A third position supports implementing a long-term moratorium on cloning research until the scientific, ethical, and social issues have been fully debated. Without a moratorium, it is entirely likely that new research discoveries could outpace discussion and thereby change the issues under debate. Both issues of cloning research on pre-embryos and cloning human beings should be subjected to ethical and theological scrutiny as well as tests of political and legal feasibility. Christians bring to this social discussion an emphasis on human creative possibility, to be sure, but also a "suspicion" (Nelson) that stresses human fallibility, misplaced self-confidence, and the risks of arrogance.

Prohibitions. A fourth position places cloning within the context of positive eugenics and offers a critique of both research process and product based on the ethical precedents and prohibitions established with respect to genetic enhancements. In particular, cloning raises issues about the substantive characteristics desired in a person, the control of enormous powers of manipulation by a very small circle of experts, and whether human life will assume instrumental rather than inherent value.

Cloning Research: *Green/Amber*

Human Cloning: *Amber*

PROTESTANT CHRISTIANITY: CONSERVATIVE EVANGELICAL

The diversity of Protestantism is illustrated by the different views of Joseph Fletcher (Episcopal) and Paul Ramsey (Methodist) on human cloning. This report will try to illuminate some of the diversity while avoiding oversimplification by distinguishing between conservative evangelical and mainline Protestantism.

The conservative evangelical denominations considered in this report account for some 15% of the American religious population. This includes the largest Protestant body, the Southern

Baptist Convention (SBC), which claims over 16 million adherents. The Christian Life Commission of the SBC issued a resolution against human cloning on 6 March 1997. While evangelical theologians and denominations do not speak as one voice, they are united in relying heavily on the Bible as the principal authority for spiritual and moral life. Protestant evangelicals began to take a serious interest in biomedical ethics following the Roe v. Wade decision legalizing abortion in 1973, and their writings continue to focus on ethical questions at the beginning and ending of life. However, partly as a response to the influence of secular, philosophical models in medicine, evangelical ethicists have begun to address all the major questions of biomedical ethics.

The Sanctity of Life. Given evangelical emphasis on the sanctity of human life, it is not surprising that J. Kerby Anderson, perhaps the first evangelical author to address human cloning, set it within the context of the right-to-life controversy. Anderson argued that the sanctity of life is violated by cloning in two different ways. First, cloning research would inevitably result in loss of embryonic life. Secondly, although Anderson believes a clone would have a soul, he holds that societal disregard for the sanctity of human life would lead to a re-definition of humanity. In that way, society could treat the clone as a repository for spare organs and tissues.

Parenthood. Evangelical discourse affirms the intrinsic connection between marriage and parenthood delineated in the *Genesis* creation story. Human cloning is theologically misguided because it breaks this connection so completely. In so doing, cloning no less ruptures critical connections between parent and child. Gilbert Meilaender argues that a marital context of giving and receiving in love is the ideal context for procreation and nurture of a child. This relational context is emphatically severed in human cloning, which "aims directly at the heart of the mystery that is the child." Thus, the idea of a child as a "gift" is diminished as the child becomes both a project and a projection of the self.

Southern Baptist scholars portray human cloning as distinctive and discontinuous from previous methods of human procreation; indeed, it is represented as a "radical break with the human past, and with the established patterns of human life." The distinctiveness of cloning is manifested in what R. Albert Mohler, Jr., refers to as "consumer eugenics" in which "direct genetic customization" of the human embryo is performed. Moreover, the secular principles of procreative liberty and autonomy that support

133

cloning assault the integrity and social necessity of the family and of marital love: "The possibility of human cloning allows for the final emancipation of human reproduction from the marital relationship. Indeed, cloning would allow for the emancipation of human reproduction from any relationship" (Mohler, Jr.).

The Image of God. Evangelical authors directly connect issues of diminished humanity and relationality embedded in human cloning with a violation of the *imago Dei*.

Religious thinkers within the Southern Baptist Convention also invoke the *imago Dei* as a bar against human cloning. As bearers of this image, human beings gain insight into self-understanding and human uniqueness and receive a distinctive status relative to the rest of creation. This sacred uniqueness is compromised by efforts at human cloning. On 6 March 1997, the Christian Life Commission of the Southern Baptist Convention issued a resolution entitled "Against Human Cloning" that supported the decision of President Clinton to prohibit federal funding for human cloning research and requested "that the Congress of the United States make human cloning unlawful." The resolution also called on "all nations of the world to make efforts to prevent the cloning of any human being."

Evangelical ethicists contend that cloning can contradict human creativity and innovation embedded in the image of God, rather than express it (as claimed by some mainline Protestant theologians). Instead of reflecting an openness to the future, cloning in fact involves a replication of the past. Thus, it should not be interpreted as creative but rather as "reactionary biological conservatism" (Jones). Cloning perpetuates the past and thereby belies our unwillingness to accept contingency and the unknown.

Cloning Research. Research on the human pre-embryo is assessed as "immoral." Echoing Ramsey's concern, evangelical authors describe cloning as an immoral experiment on a person without his or her consent. Moreover, cloning procedures are likely to ensue in embryonic death due to abnormalities in the embryo or practical difficulties in transferring the embryo to a host womb.

Cloning Research: *Red*

Human Cloning: *Red*

ROMAN CATHOLIC CHRISTIANITY

The Roman Catholic Church is the largest denomination in the U.S., with approximately 40% of the religious population and over 20% of the general population. The religious and moral authority for Roman Catholicism is grounded in the witness of God and Jesus Christ in the Bible, as interpreted through the teaching office (magisterium) of the Church. In the United States, Roman Catholic teaching is coordinated by the National Conference of Catholic Bishops (NCCB). Roman Catholic theologians, though not always in agreement with magisterial teaching, have been among the most influential contributors in biomedical ethics, and have addressed the possibility of human cloning since the 1960s.

National Conference of Catholic Bishops. In the United States, the NCCB released a statement in March 1997 rejecting human cloning on several grounds, including an appeal to the rights of children to have real parents and to not be manufactured as copies. Moreover, research involving the cloning of human embryos is deemed unethical due to its risks and non-therapeutic objectives. The NCCB also issued support for the testimony of John Cardinal O'Connor before the New York State Senate (13 March 1997). Cardinal O'Connor criticized cloning as contrary to human parenthood and human wisdom. Human cloning violates the norms of procreation and parenthood through a process that removes "the humanism from human parents and the human child."

A serious survey of the state of our degraded external environment reveals that human beings lack the wisdom to experiment with the internal human environment. O'Connor emphasizes in particular questions of technical inefficiency and issues of the character and qualifications of those who would direct the research and process of cloning, concluding that these are not matters to be left to technical specialists. O'Connor also observes that cloning falls beyond the parameters of the vocation of medicine: "The act of human cloning itself cures no pathology. Thus, we are not doctoring the patient but doctoring the race." While Roman Catholicism encourages scientific development in the service of the person and human dignity, proposals for research "that are hostile to human parenthood, unknown in deleterious consequences, and cure no disease...are not medicine and are not welcome."

135

Theologians: Cloning Research. While many Roman Catholic theologians have addressed the subject of human cloning, Richard A. McCormick, S.J., has provided the most constant Catholic commentary on cloning. His themes will be used as illustrative of the central concerns of theologians within the tradition. McCormick has invoked the themes of sanctity, wholeness, and individuality in criticizing cloning research on human pre-embryos. Cloning is not merely a question of scientific technique, but also involves matters of the public interest. McCormick is concerned that such research will erode respect for the human pre-embryo and prenascent life, and diminish the wonder of human diversity and uniqueness.

Parenthood. McCormick has also argued that human cloning is contrary to the meaning of marriage and the family. The purpose of marriage includes the binding of the unitive and procreative purposes of sexuality. Reproductive technologies, including cloning, suggest that embodiment is extrinsic rather than intrinsic to personhood. Such procedures depersonalize the family, "debodify" marital love, and violate the sacramental covenant of marriage. Moreover, natural law encompasses duties for both procreation and education of offspring; parental nurture is required to enable a child to develop morally and spiritually and to assume interpersonal commitments.

Roman Catholic theologians have emphasized the sins of pride and self-interest, and the human conditions of finitude and fallibility, in assessing the prospects of human cloning. However, avoiding pride should not mean falling into the sin of sloth. Human beings have a divine responsibility for dominion that can be expanded through justified scientific research.

Cloning Research: *Red*

Human Cloning: *Red*

ORTHODOX CHRISTIANITY

In the United States, the tradition of Orthodox Christianity is institutionalized in two prominent denominational bodies, the Greek Orthodox Archdiocese of America, and the Orthodox Church in America. About three% of the U.S. religious population is affiliated with these denominations. The Bible and the wisdom of the tradition provide grounds for the ecclesiastical teaching content of Orthodox Christianity. Theologians within both denominations, as well as the Orthodox Church in America itself, have addressed the subject of cloning.

The Image of God. The concept of the person within Orthodox tradition is rooted in the *imago Dei*, with the ultimate purpose of life to realize *theosis*, or God-likeness, in union and communion with others. The image of God influences judgments about reproductive technologies and cloning. Reproductive technologies used outside the context of marriage may be viewed as attempts to recreate human beings in man's image and preferred characteristics, rather than God's image. One theologian, while acknowledging the tremendous promise that cloning holds out for agricultural development, indicates that it must be condemned "as grotesque genetic manipulation when practiced on human beings."

The image of God is also invoked as the central theological claim in a public statement on cloning, issued on 11 March 1997 by the Orthodox Church in America. The Orthodox Church believes cloning use will inevitably be abused, through such examples as "the commercialization of 'prime' DNA, production of children for the purpose of providing 'spare parts,' and movement toward creation of a 'superior' class of human beings." The statement concludes with an emphatic request that "a government ban be imposed on all forms of experimentation to produce human clones and that government funding for such activity be denied." This does not preclude public support and funding for animal cloning to produce therapeutic medical products. The call for a prohibition is addressed directly to publicly-funded research, whether animal or human embryonic, that is developed for the purpose of human cloning.

Cloning Research. Orthodox theologians extend the dignity and respect owed to the person to the human embryo. This does not depend on a claim about ensoulment, but rather exhibits human finitude and fallability: "We must treat the developing embryo with dignity and respect because we do not know when it becomes a person" (Demopulos). Moreover, the inefficiency of current cloning techniques, if applied to human embryos, would constitute a tragic loss of potential human life. Such positions necessarily preclude cloning research on the embryo.

Cloning Research: *Red*

Human Cloning: *Red*

AFRICAN AMERICAN CHURCHES

Faith traditions in the African American religious community comprise approximately 11% of religious adherents in the United States. The African American churches, stemming from Methodist and Baptist traditions, locate themselves within the "black Christian tradition." This tradition is united by commitment to a fundamental principle of human equality before God, often phrased as "the parenthood of God and the kinship of all peoples." The principle offers a theological basis for criticism of racism and sexism and necessitates social reform through non-violent measures and religious witness.

Social Context. The black Christian tradition understands the history of research abuses of African Americans at the hands of medicine, such as the Tuskegee experiments, as a violation of the fundamental principle of human equality. Moreover, due to ongoing racism in society and medicine, it maintains the prospects for further exploitation of African Americans through cloning research are substantial. "The history of scientific abuse and medical neglect carries with it a legacy that is permanently imprinted upon...the collective consciousness" of African Americans (Secundy).

Given this history of past abuses, society should assume a posture of greater vigilance for minority communities. Preston N. Williams, a participant in the 1970s discussion of cloning, argues both that public oversight is necessary with respect to cloning, and that it also must be "race conscious," lest the African American community experience further marginalization within biomedical science and society (Williams).

Accountability and Education. While technology is not morally objectionable *per se,* applications of technology within this social context can be morally indefensible. Of particular concern are entrepreneurial efforts in biomedicine that are motivated by private interest and supported by concerns for commercial profit and/or racism. At a minimum, strong regulations that build in public accountability must be developed by legislative bodies to protect vulnerable patients and families from coerced choices or economic inducements. In addition, the scientific research community should voluntarily adopt strict protocols and monitoring. Communal distrust of scientific and research institutions and suspicion of commercial endeavors also entails a more comprehensive policy approach than oversight and accountability.

Embryo Research and Therapy. African American churches affirm, along with elements of historical Christianity, that human life begins at conception. The use of human embryos for medical research is problematic since it involves experimentation on living human embryos rather than embryonic material. In addition, the tradition is concerned about the procedures required for creating embryos and those used in discarding embryos. A minimal criterion of moral acceptability is therapeutic intent: Cloning of human cells, for example, should not be allowed to benefit any individual racial or ethnic group "outside of the context of a clearly identified, morally defensible, medically justifiable" condition that would benefit from such technology (Robinson).

Fairness. The tradition also raises questions about fairness and social priorities in resource allocation. The history of medical progress has often meant that African Americans assume the heaviest burdens and receive the least benefit for participation. Moreover, scientific energies and public monies used to support cloning could divert attention from diseases specific to the African American community, or from poor health indices, such as high premature birth or infant mortality rates. The principle of human equality is violated when a new area of research investigation is opened up, while many within the African American community do not have access to basic health care.

African American churches do not have any objections to the use of reproductive technologies *per se* as a means of bringing children into the world. However, the principle of equality is invoked to criticize selective access to reproductive technologies, particularly to the exclusion of African Americans. Rev. Geoffrey Ellis, president of the NAACP Interdenominational Coalition, contends that those with the technical capacity to clone "certainly will make more people like them. This certainly rules out more people like me" (Ellis). If financial resources dictate access to human cloning services, members of the black Christian tradition may experience further social marginalization. Human cloning may therefore, perpetuate social stratification rather than affirm human equality.

Cloning Research: *Flashing Red*

Human Cloning: *Red*

BIBLIOGRAPHY

Books and Documents

Anderson, J. Kerby. **Genetic Engineering,** Grand Rapids, MI: Zondeman Publishing House, 1982.

Congregation for the Doctrine of the Faith, **Instruction on Respect for Human Life in Its Origin and on the Dignity of Procreation,** Vatican City, 22 February 1987.

Doerflinger, Richard. "Remarks in Response to News Reports on the Cloning of Mammals," **National Conference of Catholic Bishops,** 25 February 1997.

Feinberg, John S., Paul D. Feinberg. **Ethics for a Brave New World,** Wheaton, IL: Crossway Books, 1993.

Fletcher, Joseph. **Humanhood: Essays in Biomedical Ethics,** Buffalo, NY: Prometheus Books, 1979; **The Ethics of Genetic Control,** Garden City, NY: Anchor, 1974; "New Beginnings in Life: A Theologian's Response," in **The New Genetics and the Future of Man,** Michael Hamilton (ed.), Grand Rapids, MI: Wm. B. Eerdmans Publishing, 1972, 78-89.

Jones, D. Gareth. **Brave New People: Ethical Issues at the Commencement of Life,** Grand Rapids, MI: Wm. B. Eerdmans Publishing, 1985.

Keown, Damien. **Buddhism and Bioethics,** New York: St. Martin's Press, 1995.

Kimbrell, Andrew. **The Human Body Shop: The Engineering and Marketing of Life,** New York: HarperCollins Publishers, 1993.

Lewis, C.S. **The Abolition of Man,** New York: Macmillan Publishing Co., 1973.

McCormick, Richard A., S.J. **How Brave a New World: Dilemmas in Bioethics,** Garden City, New York: Doubleday & Company, Inc., 1981.

O'Donovan, Oliver. **Begotten or Made?** Oxford: Clarendon Press, 1984.

Orthodox Church in America. "Statement on Recent Developments in Cloning Technology," 11 March 1997.

Ramsey, Paul. **Fabricated Man: The Ethics of Genetic Control,** New Haven: Yale University Press, 1970, esp. pp. 60-103, "Shall We Clone a Man?;" "Moral and Religious Implications of Genetic Control," in **Genetics and the Future of Man,** John D. Roslansky (ed.), New York: Appleton-Century-Croffs, 1966, 107-169.

Rosner, Fred. **Modern Medicine and Jewish Ethics,** New York: Yeshiva University Press, 1986.

World Council of Churches. **Faith and Science in an Unjust World,** Geneva: World Council of Churches, 1979.

Magazines and Newspapers

American Medical News. "No Cloning for Now: Ethics Panel," 06/02/97, 2.

Annas, George J. "Human Cloning," **ABA Journal,** May 1997, 80.

Begley, Sharon. "Little Lamb, Who MadeThee?" **Bulletin** with **Newsweek,** 03/11/97, 62.

British Medical Journal. "United States Panel Recommends Legal Ban on Human Cloning," 06/14/97, 1710.

Bruni, Frank. "Experts Urge No Hasty Curbs on Cloning," **New York Times,** 03/14/97, B2.

Butler, Declan. "Calls for Human Cloning Ban 'Stem from Ignorance,'" **Nature,** 05/22/97, 324.

Callahan, Daniel. "A Step Too Far," **New York Times,** 02/26/97, A23.

Callahan, Sidney. "Are 'Pre-Embryos' Human?" **Commonweal,** 06/20/97, 6.

Carey, John. "Cloning Wars," **Business Week,** 09/01/97, 45.

Christian Century. "Clinton Urges Ban on Cloning of Humans," 06/18/97, 19.

Christian Century. "Cloning of Embryos Stirs Ethical Concerns," 11/10/93, 1117.

Clinton, William J. "Remarks Announcing the Prohibition of Federal Funding for Cloning of Human Beings and an Exchange," **Weekly Compilation of Presidential Documents,** 03/10/97, 278.

Coupland, Douglas. "Clone, Clone on the Range," **Time,** 03/10/97, 74.

Fielding, Ellen Wilson. "Fear of Cloning," **Human Life Review,** Spring 1997, 15.

Fiore, Mark. "Clinton Proposes Legislation to Ban Research on Cloning of Humans," **Chronicle of Higher Education,** 06/20/97, A32.

Free Inquiry. "Declaration in Defense of Cloning and the Integrity of Scientific Research," Summer 1997, 11.

Gibson, Nevil. "Leave Human Clones Alone Say Suspicious Kiwis," **National Business Review,** 05/30/97, 16.

Gorman, Christine. "To Ban or Not to Ban?" **Time,** 06/16/97, 66.

Gross, Jane. "Thinking Twice About Cloning," **New York Times,** 02/27/97, B1.

Hernandez, Raymond. "A Ban on Human Cloning Is Urged," **New York Times,** 02/26/97, B5.

Holden, Constance. "Calf Cloned from Bovine Cell Line," **Science,** 08/15/97, 903.

Journal of the American Medical Association. "Opposition to Human Cloning Grows," 06/11/97, 1750.

Kass, Leon R. "The Wisdom of Repugnance," **New Republic,** 06/02/97, 17.

Kevles, Daniel J. "Study Cloning, But Don't Ban It," **New York Times,** 02/26/97, A23.

Kleiner, Kurt. "Dolly Starts a Stampede in Congress," **New Scientist,** 03/15/97, 4.

Kilner, John F. "Stop Cloning Around," **Christianity Today,** April 28, 1997, 10.

Kolata, Gina. "Ethics Panel Recommends a Ban on Human Cloning," **New York Times,** 06/07/97, 22.

Kolata, Gina. "For Some Infertility Experts, Human Cloning Is a Dream," **New York Times,** 06/07/97, 8.

Kolata, Gina. "Rush Is on for Cloning of Animals," **New York Times,** 06/03/97, C8.

Langreth, Robert. "Cloning Has Fascinating, Disturbing Potential," **Wall Street Journal,** 02/24/97, B1.

Latham, Stephen R. "The Clone Age," **ABA Journal,** July 1997, 68.

Leutwyler, Kristin. "Still Cloning Around," **Scientific American,** Oct. 1997, 32.

Macklin, Ruth. "Human Cloning? Don't Just Say No," **U.S. News & World Report,** 03/10/97, 64.

Marshall, Eliot. "Mammalian Cloning Debate Heats Up," **Science,** 03/21/97, 1733.

Marwick, Charles. "Put Human Cloning on Hold, Say Bioethicists," **Journal of the American Medical Association,** 07/02/97, 13.

National Review, "Cloning Cloning Cloning," 03/24/97, 16.

Nature. "WHO Chief Defends Use of Animal Models," 03/20/97, 204.

New Scientist. "A Triumph of Hope," 05/31/97, 3.

New York Times. "Cloning for Good or Evil," 02/25/97, A26.

New York Times. "Southern Baptists Seek Ban on Cloning Humans," 06/20/97, A20.

Palca, J. "A Reliable Animal Model for AIDS," **Science,** 06/01/90, 1078.

Pendick, Daniel. "Clones Unlimited," **New Scientist,** 08/16/97, 11.

Post, Stephen G. "The Judeo-Christian Case Against Human Cloning," **America,** 06/21/97, 19.

Praded, Joni. "Cloning: The Missing Debate," **Animals,** May/June, 1997, 21.

Robertson, John A. "The Question of Human Cloning," **Hastings Center Report,** March/April 1994, 6.

Schorr, Daniel. "The Clonal Man," **New Leader,** March 24, 1997, 5.

Seelye, Katharine Q. "G.O.P. Lawmaker Proposes Bill to Ban Human Cloning," **New York Times,** 03/06/97, B12.

Seppa, N. "Clinton Calls for Ban on Human Cloning," **Science News,** 06/14/97, 367.

Shapiro, Harold T. "Ethical and Policy Issues of Human Cloning," **Science,** 07/11/97, 195.

Thornton, Gus W. "The Cloning Conundrum," **Animals,** May/June, 1997, 3.

USA Today Magazine. "Producing Identical Pigs for Research," June 1993, 3.

USA Today Magazine. "This Little Piggy Is a Clone," June 1992, 5.

Wadman, Meredith. "Cloning for Research 'Should Be Allowed,'" **Nature,** 07/03/97, 6.

Wadman, Meredith. "Politicians Accused of 'Shooting from the Hip' on Human Cloning," **Nature,** 03/13/97, 97.

Wadman, Meredith. "Republicans Seek to Widen Cloning Ban," **Nature,** 06/19/97, 748.

Wall Street Journal – Eastern Edition. "House Panel Votes to Ban Funds for Clone Research," 07/30/97, B6.

Wall Street Journal – Eastern Edition. "Scottish Institute Seeks Patents for Cloning Process," 05/09/97, B2.

Watson, Rory. "European Parliament Wants World Ban on Human Cloning," **British Medical Journal,** 03/22/97, 847.

Watson, Traci. "Cloning a Flap Over Research," **U.S. News & World Report,** 03/17/97, 36.

Wright, Susan. "After Dolly, a Slippery Ban on Human Cloning," **Christian Science Monitor,** 06/23/97, 19.

INDEX

143